The Complete Guide to Pickling

The Complete Guide to
Pickling

Pickle and Ferment Everything
Your Garden or Market Has to Offer

Julie Laing

Photography by Andrew Purcell

ROCKRIDGE
PRESS

Interior and Cover Designer: Scott Petrower
Art Producer: Meg Baggott
Editor: Cecily McAndrews
Production Editor: Rachel Taenzler
Photography © 2020 Andrew Purcell. Food styling by Carrie Purcell.
Author photo courtesy of Brenda Ahearn Photography.

ISBN: Print 978-1-64739-360-1 | eBook 978-1-64739-361-8
R1

To Grandma Tiny, who believed I could do anything. To my mother, who taught me to love homemade food. And to George, who enthusiastically samples each jar.

Contents

Introduction

I have pickle brine in my blood.

My father and his father grew large gardens, intending to eat the fruits and vegetables of their labor as pickles. My paternal grandparents kept a large crock on the back porch with a rock weighing down its aromatic kraut; pickled relishes and other home-canned goodies filled their storeroom shelves. On my mother's side, my uncle experimented with fiery mustards, and the siblings and cousins of that generation swapped recipe cards as if they were baseball cards.

Growing up, my own family's kitchen turned into a processing center every summer, with my mom manning the canning kettle and my grandmother, sister, and I cleaning and chopping bucketloads of vegetables and fruit that would see us through winter.

When I reached college, I realized that my homemade history was delicious in a way no university cafeteria could ever touch. So I began to build and share my own recipe collection. I also became an intrepid traveler, visiting markets as often as museums. I discovered the difference between American and British pickles while living in London. I tasted my first dill-laden gravlax in Norway, pickled young ginger in Japan, brined mushrooms in Russia, salt-preserved lemons in Morocco, and fermented fruits in the South Pacific. Every time I returned home, I was determined to re-create the flavors in my kitchen.

My kitchen has been in northwest Montana for years. Living here lets me follow in my father's footsteps, growing in the ultrashort summer season most of the produce my husband and I eat all year. Storing this bounty in our 500-square-foot cabin requires creativity, with canning shelves lining the mudroom, a mini freezer stuffed to the brim, and reinforced refrigerator shelves supporting gallons of ferments. This description seems overwhelming, but I find joy and relaxation in growing and preserving much of what I eat.

That joy inspired me to start *Twice as Tasty*, a food blog where I write about how to eat well year-round. Over the years, the blog has grown to include hundreds of recipes. It has sprouted in-person workshops and other projects, including the book you now hold.

This book includes some of my favorite pickling recipes, including ones modernized from family recipes and others adopted from my travels. The collection has something for everyone. If you're making your first pickle, the easiest recipes, particularly those in chapter 2, come together in just a few minutes and use staples and tools that are likely already in your kitchen. But experienced pickle lovers can expand their repertoire with both classic and tantalizing new flavors. If your storage space is limited, many recipes let you make a jar at a time. On the other end, gardeners can use the large-batch recipes for both canning and fermenting to preserve bumper crops and then enjoy them all year.

Every recipe in this book has been designed to ensure a safe and delicious pickle. As a professional writer and editor, I take facts and sources seriously; as a food geek, my history is long and well documented. I've relied on research and lab-tested results to calculate each recipe in this book. Where I introduced variation, I checked trusted sources to ensure food safety. For good measure, I tested such recipes with a ThermoWorks high-accuracy pH meter.

I hope you enjoy the results. Be inspired to try new-to-you flavors. And let me know what you think: You can find me at TwiceasTasty.com, @twiceastastyblog on Instagram, and the Twice as Tasty Community on Facebook. Happy pickling!

1

Getting Started

This chapter launches you on your pickling adventures, whether you are making your first pickle or are a practiced hand trying a new style. You'll learn about types of pickles and their origins, as well as key ingredients and tools. The chapter explains the differences between fresh pickles preserved by the acidity of vinegar and fermented pickles cured in salt. Gardeners will find tips on growing produce for pickling, and flavor-savvy readers will discover ways to use pickle brine. As you explore the recipes in the rest of this book, use this chapter as a reference guide for, among other things, step-by-step canning and fermentation instructions and troubleshooting solutions.

A Brief History of Pickling

If your image of pickles features toxic-green waffle-cut chips on fast-food burgers, you're in for a brilliant surprise with this book. People were making pickles long before fast-food chains, or even America, existed. Some sources point to Mesopotamians as the originators of pickles, around 2400 BCE; among other foods, they were preserving cucumbers imported from India. Other sources trace the oldest known style of pickle, using miso, to Asia. Miso itself is a fermented food made from soybeans. The first pickles were surely fermented, one of the simplest, and oldest, ways of preserving food. Fermentation requires no special tools, environment, or heat—just a vessel and, ideally, salt.

Christopher Columbus was likely the first importer of pickles to America, along with the techniques for making them; pickles outlasted fresh food on voyages, and their creation was common household knowledge in the pre-refrigeration era. After government researchers developed a commercial pasteurization process for shelf-stable pickles in the 1930s, vinegar-preserved cucumbers began to take over the US pickle market.

This technique of using vinegar to prevent spoilage has many advantages over fermentation: It's faster, easier to control, and allows adjustments to texture and saltiness. But the simplicity of vinegar-based pickles also leads to a less varied flavor profile. Fermented cucumber pickles, with their crisp texture and complex flavor, outshine even the best cucumbers pickled in vinegar. That's why fermentation and other traditional pickling processes have been growing in popularity.

What Is a Pickle, Anyway?

Whether you like them tangy or sour, a pickle is a food that has been preserved with acid. Tangy-tasting pickles tend to be preserved using vinegar. These fresh pickles can be made using a quick, refrigerated, or canned process. Pickles typically described as "sour" undergo a process called lacto-fermentation that uses salt to create acidity.

A WORLD OF PICKLES

Rich pickling traditions throughout the world inspired this book's recipes, letting you travel the globe without leaving your table. The recipe chapters open with Sunomono, Japanese pickles familiar to sushi fans (page 28). The book also includes several variations on Korean kimchi (pages 92–99) and Thai and Chinese sauces (such as Sambal Oelek, page 132, and Scratch-Made Sriracha, page 130). From Eastern European and Russian kitchens come the scents of hearty, flavorful pickled foods such as Sauerkraut (page 86), Kvashenaya Kapusta (Russian-Inspired Soured Cabbage, page 88), and Russian-Inspired Pickled Mushrooms (page 40), while summer vegetables (including Summer Giardiniera, page 71, and Romesco-Style Roasted Pepper Sauce, page 145) and pickled fish (Escabeche-Style Fish, page 180, and Gravlax, page 178) tempt you into the Mediterranean and Scandinavia.

In warm climates, tropical fruits dominate, from Preserved Lemons (page 109) in Morocco to Tepache (page 188) made from pineapple rind in Mexico. Throughout Latin America, light, spicy sauces and pickles also brighten meals, including curtido in El Salvador (pages 35 and 100) and simple Spicy Vinegar in Puerto Rico (page 128).

Fresh Pickles

When you make a fresh pickle, you're likely using a type of vinegar to preserve it, or perhaps another acid like lemon juice. Fresh pickles can range from a quick-pickled salad with sushi to a jar of pickled garlic in your refrigerator to a shelf-stable quart of cucumber dills.

Counterintuitively, you can *can* fresh pickles. Proper portions of vinegar (or other acid) make them safe for long-term storage, and they lack the probiotics of fermented pickles that can be destroyed by the canning process (more on that later).

Fresh pickles can be further divided (as I've done in this book) by how soon you can enjoy them and how long they last: Quick pickles are ready and generally should be eaten within 1 to 2 days. You'll find a whole chapter of such recipes starting on page 27. Refrigerated pickles should sit at least 2 days before you dig into them, but they often last weeks to months, as explained in the recipes starting on page 55. Canned pickles usually taste best if you store them at least a few weeks and eat them within a year. For the step-by-step process for canning pickles, see page 6.

Fermented Pickles

For fermented pickles, salt is front and center in the preservation process. Lacto-fermentation is essentially souring via microbes. It lets the good bacteria that are naturally present in vegetables and fruit thrive. These microorganisms break down the sugars and carbohydrates in food, causing a chemical change that increases acidity and ultimately preserves the food. The process creates a bold, sour flavor.

Properly fermented food looks, smells, and tastes bright and crisp. In addition, ferments are touted as being easily digestible and highly nutritious. They develop intricate flavor profiles thanks to the lactic and acetic acids, alcohol, carbon dioxide, and other compounds produced by the fermentation process. That process breaks down complex proteins into readily digestible amino acids, and it builds up new nutrients, particularly B vitamins. Just as many types of vegetables and fruit can be fermented as can be pickled in vinegar: cucumbers, asparagus, onions, snap beans, watermelon rind, and more. The "Fermentation, Step by Step" section (page 9) covers the basics of fermenting.

To Can or Not to Can?

That is the question. The answer has everything to do with acidity. Pickles are acidic by definition, and high-acid food can be safely canned in a boiling-water bath. So why should you can some pickles but not others?

The first reason is degree of acidity: To be safely stored at room temperature, processed food needs a pH of 4.6 or lower. Otherwise, bacteria can grow. Every food you pickle has a different natural pH, which means it needs a different minimum amount of vinegar (acetic acid) in the jar to ensure an overall safe pH. That's why you follow canning recipes; they've been calculated to ensure enough acid to stop bacteria.

The second reason is quality: Some pickles taste better and crisper when unheated. This includes quick pickles, which rapidly infuse flavor, and fermented pickles, which retain probiotic benefits and crispness if unprocessed. But other pickled foods can withstand the heat treatment or don't need a crispy texture; these include snap beans, relishes, and chutneys.

This book makes it easy for you. Each recipe gives the process that creates the best pickle for that base ingredient. If a recipe can be canned, you'll find the *Can This* label and the key steps in the recipe's instructions or tips. If you're new to or need a refresher on water-bath canning, see the step-by-step instructions coming up next.

Canning, Step by Step

Canning is a process, not a mystery: If you can follow directions, you can get it right. The US Department of Agriculture's *Complete Guide to Home Canning*, available online, gives government-approved guidelines. The steps here reflect the USDA's pickling process for boiling-water-bath canning.

Step 1: Read Your Recipe

Read the whole recipe before you start. To kill food spoilers, including spores that cause botulism, and to form an airtight seal that blocks new bacteria, use the ingredients and tools specified in the recipe.

Step 2: Gather and Prepare Your Supplies

Start with fresh produce, ideally taking it straight from your garden or a local farmer to your kitchen for pickling. Gather your equipment and check its condition. Ensure the canning jars are free from chips or cracks, the rings are not rusted or bent, and the lids are new and unused.

Set the rack in the canner, fill it halfway with water, and bring it to a near boil. Fill and heat a teakettle in case you need more boiling water. If you have hard water, add ½ teaspoon of distilled vinegar to the water bath to help keep the jar exteriors clean.

Wash the jars, rings, and lids with hot, soapy water, then rinse well; keep the jars hot. Leave rings and lids at room temperature unless the manufacturer's packaging says otherwise.

Check the recipe's processing time. If that time, before your altitude adjustment (see "All about Altitude," page 191), is under 10 minutes, sanitize the jars: Fill the canner with water and add the jars, ensuring the water remains at least 1 inch above their tops. Bring to a boil and set the timer for 10 minutes.

Step 3: Prepare Your Ingredients

While the canner heats, make your pickles as instructed. Pay attention to the vinegar's acidity (the percentage on your bottle must match or be higher than the one in the recipe) and the quantities of all ingredients.

Avoid changing a canning recipe. Altering the vinegar, water, and primary ingredients can affect the pH, as can boiling longer than specified. By following the recipe, you can feel confident that your beautiful, properly stored jars are shelf-stable until you pop them open.

Step 4: Fill Your Jars

When ready, quickly fill each hot jar; a wide-mouth funnel reduces mess. Leave the headspace—the room between the food surface and the jar's rim—indicated in the recipe. Pickles generally need ½ inch of headspace, but check the recipe for specifics.

Remove any air bubbles by inserting a bamboo or wooden chopstick down the jar's inner edge, pressing it up and down while turning the jar. Wipe the jar's rim clean with a cloth or paper towel dampened with water or distilled vinegar.

Place the lid, then screw on the ring until just finger-tight. Avoid cranking down. Air needs to escape as the jar seals, so turn the lid until you just feel resistance. Set the jar upright in the canner using a jar lifter, then fill the next jar. Add boiling water as needed to keep at least 1 inch covering the jars.

Step 5: Take Time to Process

Cover the canner, turn the heat to high, and wait until the water fully boils. Once boiling, set the timer as specified in the recipe, adding your altitude adjustment (see "All about Altitude," page 191). Keep the canner covered and at a full boil until the timer goes off. Then turn off the heat, remove the canner lid, and wait 5 minutes.

Step 6: Store Your Jars

Use the jar lifter to move the jars to a towel-covered surface. Let cool at room temperature, without pressing the lids or retightening the rings, for at least 12 hours; the lids will ping as they seal.

After 12 hours, remove and wash the rings and wipe down the jars with a damp cloth. Label each jar, listing at least the contents and date.

Test the seal on each jar by pressing the center of the lid. If the lid flexes, replace the ring and refrigerate the unsealed jar for immediate use. If the jar is sealed, store it in a cool, dark, dry place; leave the ring off so that it doesn't rust or trap food particles. For the best flavor and texture, eat the pickles within a year.

EIGHT USES FOR PICKLING BRINE

Instead of pouring your leftover pickle brine down the drain, give it a second life. Brine holds electrolytes, minerals, and even probiotics, as well as loads of flavor, so extend its use with any of the following applications:

1. **Bake it.** Home cheese-makers have long replaced water with whey in bread recipes, and pickle lovers make similar substitutions with brine when baking rye and other breads. Try this with the brine from Half-Sour Dill Pickles (page 104).

2. **Cook it.** Braise vegetables or meats or replace a dish's vinegar with brine. Remember that vinegar brines are usually diluted and salt brines are, well, salty, so you may need to alter the recipe's liquids and sodium. Try using a couple of tablespoons of Red Onions in Wine Vinegar brine (page 42).

3. **Dress it.** Brines have many of the same components as salad dressings; just whisk in oil until emulsified. Pour the instant dressing over greens or just-cooked potatoes. Try this with Pickled Avocado Slices brine (page 32).

4. **Drink it.** A little brine goes a long way in beverages. Use fruit brines much like shrubs, sweetening the brine as needed and mixing it with seltzer or into a cocktail. Splash savory brines into cocktails for a dirty martini or souped-up Bloody Mary and garnish with Spiced Fermented Pearl Onions (page 112).

5. **Marinate it.** Many marinades have vinegar, salt, and seasonings, exactly what's left after you empty a pickle jar. Add a little oil before pouring over halibut, chicken, or feta. Try this with Herbes de Provence Zucchini brine (page 82).

6. **Pour it.** Vinegar brine is just infused vinegar, so drizzle it over vegetables or set it out as a dipping sauce. Spicy brines can be used like hot sauce. Try this with Chile Rings brine (page 45).

7. **Refill it.** Some brines can be used again. Miso beds in particular can be multi-use (such as Misozuke, page 73). Quick-pickle brines retain most of their acidity, making them refill candidates. Use only fresh brines for fermentation and canning to ensure safe pH levels.

8. **Sauce it.** Stir some brine into cream for an Alfredo sauce with zing or add brine to caramelized sugar and reduce the mixture to a flavorful gastrique. Try this with the brine from Mushrooms Pickled in White Wine (page 41).

The only vegetable brine I don't reuse comes from Short-Ferment Potatoes (page 118), with its high salt concentration. Plus, any brines that smell "off" or show signs of mold should be discarded.

Fermentation, Step by Step

Fermenting is about patience. You can start many ferments in minutes but won't try them for days or weeks. Fermentation happens while you wait. You're the boss, but not a micromanager; your job is to set up and maintain an effective work environment for those star employees, beneficial *Lactobacillus* bacteria.

Step 1: Gather Your Supplies

Read the entire recipe, noting times; ferments may be built in stages, with breaks for salting or compression. Ultra-fresh produce gives desirable lactobacilli their best chance of success. Wash your equipment in hot, sudsy water, then rinse well and let air-dry. Skip the antimicrobial soap; you want beneficial bacteria to thrive.

Step 2: Prepare Your Ingredients

Mise en place (preparing your ingredients) makes assembly easier. Check the recipe's yield; it indicates the ideal container size for the listed ingredients. Fermenting vessels are less standardized than canning jars, so use the given container size or scale the entire recipe up or down to fit your crock or jar.

Step 3: Salt or Brine Your Food

Fermentation can be divided into two general categories: dry salt and brine. In either case, salt drives fermentation. Too little, and harmful bacteria will move in. Too much, and beneficial bacteria won't multiply. Following the recipe will ensure the right proportions for fermentation to take place.

Krauts (including Apple and Cabbage Kraut, page 90) are typically dry-salted, drawing liquid from food. Mix the salt directly with the vegetables or fruit, let it penetrate the food and leach liquid, then pack everything into your jar or crock. Whole vegetables (like Half-Sour Dill Pickles, page 104) are usually brined, covering the food in salty water. Dissolve the salt in unchlorinated water, put all the other ingredients in your fermenting vessel, then pour in enough brine to submerge them.

Whether the recipe calls for dry salt or brine, the goal is enough salty liquid to protect the pickles from oxygen. Knowing the brine concentration for a recipe makes it easy to add brine as necessary to block oxygen (see the Brine Concentration chart on page 12).

Step 4: Weigh It Down

Weights keep fermenting food under the brine and away from oxygen. Check the recipe guidelines: You might want a cabbage leaf or cheesecloth for surface protection, a heavier weight to sink floating food, or both.

When full and weighted, your container should still have about 1 inch of space between its lip and the weight. The fruits or vegetables will release more liquid as they sit; you don't want your ferment at full pool and risk overflowing its banks. Finish the setup with a lid, preferably with an air lock that leaves space between it and the brine. See "Outfit Your Kitchen" (page 19) for weight and lid options.

Step 5: And Then You Wait!

Put the ferment in a cool, dark place. Lactobacilli work hardest between 60°F and 75°F. If your kitchen is warmer, try a basement, closet, or unheated bedroom. Most crocks automatically block light, but set glass jars in a cupboard or wrap them in a clean towel. Set a large plate underneath, in case the liquid breaches its banks. Then let the bacteria get to work.

Like any good boss, look in on your ferment regularly; daily is easy to remember and takes little time. Is your crock's water-sealed rim still full? Does your jar still have surface-to-lid headspace? Is brine still covering the food? If yes, your daily check-in is done. If no, adjust as needed, following the recipe's brine concentration. Once you master a recipe, you may not need to check in as often.

For tightly packed ferments, such as a kraut or kimchi, release large air bubbles over the first few days, so the brine and vegetables maintain direct contact. Press a long bamboo or wooden skewer or wooden spoon handle down through the mixture to the bottom of the jar several times.

When tiny bubbles appear, likely by the third day, your lactobacilli are on the job. The longer your fermentation sits, the more it develops. You'll see and smell the changes. Food color may dull, whole produce may sink, and brine will cloud. Over time, your pickles will build up several *Lactobacillus* species. More species mean more complex flavors.

Yeast species may also develop. Kahm yeast, colloquially called scum, can coat the surface, indicating your ferment needs to produce more lactic acid. This filmy layer is harmless but can lead to "off" flavors and softness; skim it off with a spoon, adding brine as needed to submerge the food. See "Pickle Troubleshooting" (page 22) for ways to encourage beneficial bacteria and solve potential problems.

Step 6: Taste and Store Your Ferment

Start tasting your pickles when indicated in the recipe. This may be days or weeks, depending on temperature, acidity, and more. The first taste test is just another check on the slow, steady progress of the lactobacilli.

Keep fermenting and sampling until the pickles reach your preferred flavor. *Done* means "I like it" with ferments, but there are some clues. Finished pickles taste more sour than salty. Whole pickles have even color throughout when cut. Cloudy brine and dull colors are normal; despite them, pickles remain crisp with a bright tanginess.

When you like the pickles, store them. Glass containers and nonreactive lids work best for long-term storage, and refrigerating slows fermentation. The stronger the flavor, the more acidic the pickle and the longer it will keep.

Check that the stored pickles remain submerged; try a light weight if they float. To store jars for more than 6 months, strain, simmer, and cool the brine, then repack everything in a clean jar to extend crispness.

BRINE CONCENTRATION

Brine strength, or the ratio of salt to water by weight, ensures proper fermentation and affects fermenting speed, taste, and storage duration.

Don't be surprised if you need to add brine to your fermentations to keep food covered and protected from oxygen exposure. The vegetable variety, fermenting temperature, and even growing conditions can affect the natural liquid in produce. In addition, skimming off surface yeast usually removes liquid.

Brine strength is as important when you top off as when you start a ferment; you'll change the balance, and perhaps its safety, if you just add water. To make extra brine, check the brine concentration given in the recipe. Then in a small measuring cup, whisk the following amount of Diamond Crystal kosher salt into 1 cup of room-temperature, unchlorinated water, stirring until the salt dissolves:

SALT VOLUME	SALT WEIGHT	BRINE CONCENTRATION
2¼ teaspoons	6 grams	2.5%
3 teaspoons	8 grams	3.5%
3¾ teaspoons	10 grams	4.25%
4½ teaspoons	12 grams	5%

Add enough brine to the fermentation jar to submerge the vegetables. Store any extra brine in a small glass jar with a nonreactive lid. To use Morton pickling salt or another salt in your brine, see the salt section in "Choosing the Right Ingredients," page 13.

Choosing the Right Ingredients

Some common ingredients appear in almost every pickling recipe. This section helps you select the best options.

Salt

Salt is crucial, especially in fermented pickles, for safe preservation. As fruit and vegetables absorb salt, they release juices, diluting the brine concentration while acidifying the food. If you're worried about your salt intake, keep in mind that when you eat a pickle, you're consuming far less salt than went into the jar.

I prefer Diamond Crystal kosher salt for pickling, followed by Morton pickling salt. Sea salt can be used when flavoring quick salsas and sauces. You can substitute Morton for Diamond Crystal, but not directly. For every tablespoon of Morton pickling salt or sea salt (16 grams), you need 2 tablespoons of Diamond Crystal kosher salt (which weighs 8 grams per tablespoon). When buying salt, look for one word in the ingredient list: *salt*. Anticaking agents and other additives can cloud brine and discolor pickles but are common in table salt and even some kosher brands, including Morton kosher salt.

Water

Water is water, right? Not always. Some water carries high concentrations of iron, lead, or trace minerals. In a public water system, tap water is likely chlorinated. These elements interfere with lactobacilli. If you don't know what's in your water, use distilled water for fermenting. Vinegar pickles aren't as picky, but choose distilled water if your tap source has known contaminants or your pickles seem discolored.

Acid

Most added-acid pickles use vinegar made from apples, wine, or grains. Choose a bottle that matches or exceeds the acidity percentage in the recipe. The dilution should be on the label.

Most pickling recipes call for vinegar with 5 percent acidity, with at least a 1:1 vinegar-to-water ratio to ensure food safety. Check labels, because US manufacturers can sell vinegar at 4 percent acidity and are increasingly doing so. Cider vinegar requires a keen eye. Look for 5 percent acidity and apples, not flavored distilled vinegar, as the base. Manufacturers have also launched "pickling vinegar," essentially premade brine with water, sugar, and salt. It cannot be safely substituted for vinegar in recipes.

In this book, when vinegars have higher (balsamic vinegar) or lower (rice vinegar) acidity, this percentage is noted, and the recipe's vinegar-to-water ratio has been calculated to ensure a safe, delicious pickle. The one vinegar you won't find is distilled white. It's great for cleaning, but I find it harsh in pickles.

Lemon or lime juice also aids pickling. When bottled, these juices bear the same dilution label as vinegars but also contain preservatives. Studies have found sufficient natural acidity in fresh lemons and limes, but these findings remain unconfirmed by the USDA. I use fresh citrus options in recipes when the juice's role is flavor, rather than preservation. You can't safely substitute Meyer lemons, a lemon–mandarin orange cross with a higher pH than *Citrus limon*.

Spices and Herbs

Spices and herbs bring many assets to the pickling game, from flavors to antioxidants. As a bonus, you can generally alter them without affecting quality and safety.

When choosing spices and herbs, buy fresh, whole, small quantities. For maximum flavor, grow your own or find a bulk source, such as a natural food store or spice shop, that regularly turns over its stock. Turmeric is the main exception; the fresh root tends to stain cutting boards and clothing, making powder a worthy (and less messy) substitute for small quantities.

When thinly slicing fresh ginger, I usually get about 18 slices per 1-inch piece. The same applies to horseradish. In the recipes, use this as a guide when the ingredients include fresh ginger and horseradish slices.

Spice blends can speed up the pickling prep process, so I've shared my favorite essential blends (page 16). To make just one recipe that calls for a particular blend, simply add its individual spices to the jar.

Pickling for Gardeners

Gardening and pickling go hand in hand. If you grow a garden, pickling is a great way to preserve bumper crops. If you love pickles, you can grow specific vegetables and fruit just to be able to stick them in brine.

Planning, Growing, and Storing

Endless resources on planning, planting, and growing can be found online, in bookstores, and through county extension services. It's tempting to take this information and a seed catalog and start designing your garden. But to preserve what you grow, I recommend working backward: Flip through this book first and then think about what you want on your shelves.

First, consider what you'll eat. Give thought to where you'll store your haul. Unless you're pickling as soon as you harvest and canning in a boiling-water bath, fresh and pickled produce needs refrigeration.

One trick manages all these factors: Start small. Choose one or two plants you love as pickles as preserving crops. Expect the unexpected bumper crop by saving space in your schedule and kitchen for additional pickles. Be inspired and try one new plant as single-jar pickles, then dedicate space to your new favorites next season.

Varieties for Pickling

Certain varieties, such as many heirlooms with savable seed, produce the tastiest, crispest pickles. Once you choose types of produce to grow, seek out these varieties for pickling:

→ **Pickling cucumbers:** Despite their popularity, cucumbers can be challenging to preserve. The recipes here share tricks to keep them crisp, but there's only one way to make a really good cucumber pickle: Start with super-fresh pickling cucumbers. Pickling cucumbers can be found in many varieties, but in all cases they are smaller, less watery, and thinner-skinned than the waxed slicing or burpless cucumbers so popular in grocery stores.

ESSENTIAL SPICE BLENDS

Makes about ½ cup per blend
Prep time: 5 minutes per blend

Spice blends can be a handy shortcut. The following blends appear in this book's recipes. Unless otherwise indicated, use fresh whole spices and other aromatics; they can last twice as long as ground spices and won't muddy brines.

BASIC DILLY SPICE BLEND

5 teaspoons yellow mustard seeds
5 teaspoons dill seeds
5 teaspoons coriander seeds
4 teaspoons black peppercorns

2 dried chiles de árbol or other small hot chiles
2 bay leaves

ULTRA PICKLING SPICE BLEND

1 tablespoon yellow mustard seeds
1 tablespoon dill seeds
1 tablespoon coriander seeds
1 tablespoon allspice berries
2 teaspoons black peppercorns
1½ teaspoons whole cloves

1 teaspoon freshly grated nutmeg
1 teaspoon dried ginger pieces
2 dried chiles de árbol or other small hot chiles
2 bay leaves
1 (3-inch) cinnamon stick

SWEET-SAVORY SPICE BLEND

6 (3-inch) cinnamon sticks
2 tablespoons allspice berries
2 tablespoons juniper berries

1 tablespoon freshly grated nutmeg
1 tablespoon whole cloves
1 tablespoon black peppercorns

MEXICAN-INSPIRED SPICE BLEND

3 tablespoons dried oregano

2 tablespoons yellow mustard seeds

2 tablespoons cumin seeds

1 tablespoon black peppercorns

16 dried chiles de árbol or other
small hot chiles

BREAD-AND-BUTTER SPICE BLEND

¼ cup yellow mustard seeds

1 tablespoon ground turmeric

1 tablespoon celery seeds

1 tablespoon ground mustard

2 teaspoons black peppercorns

2 teaspoons dried ginger pieces

1 teaspoon coriander seeds

4 dried chiles de árbol or other
small hot chiles

1. In a small glass jar, combine the ingredients for a blend, cap the jar tightly, and store it in a cool, dark place for up to 1 year.

2. To use a blend, measure the amount you need into a small, dry skillet. Place it over medium-low heat for 2 to 5 minutes, stirring constantly, until the spices are fragrant and begin to pop. Let cool to room temperature before using.

Ingredient Tip: Large whole aromatics, such as cinnamon, nutmeg, and dried chiles and ginger, can be wrapped in a dish towel and crushed with a rolling pin or kraut pounder. Smaller spices can be crushed with the side of a large knife or a mortar and pestle.

→ **Lemon cucumbers and numerous Asian varieties:** These have thin, edible skins; small seeds; and firm flesh. This can make them more appealing for quick pickles than peeled slicing cucumbers, which quickly become soft and soggy.

→ **Horseradish or grape leaves:** Freshness and other tricks in the recipes do the most to retain cucumber crispness, but horseradish and grape leaves have helpful tannins and can be used to line jars as insurance. Horseradish spreads readily, so plant it only where you really want it. The root flavors many recipes and can be pickled solo (see Vinegar-Based Horseradish Paste, page 150).

→ **Spring alliums:** Pickling can start from the season's first harvest. Spring-planted bulb onions and garlic heads won't be ready for weeks, but fall-planted (or unharvested) ones become spring crops the next season. I also recommend perennial walking onions, also called topsetting or Egyptian onions; they require no effort, just a bed to wander in as their topset bulbs fall over and self-root.

→ **Chiles:** Immediately change a pickle's heat level and flavor by using chiles. Local nurseries typically offer customer favorites, and growing from seed gives further options. Choose your preferred heat level on the Scoville scale or buy varieties to use in specific recipes, such as Fridge-Pickled Pepperoncini (page 77).

→ **Colorful vegetables:** Black cherry tomatoes, deep purple carrots, golden beets, and multicolor radishes grow easily and impress guests. Colors often fade in brine with time, so turn the brightest into quick pickles. You can also gift beautiful jars, because brine soaks up color.

Pickling has long saved large harvests, whether you intended to grow boxes of zucchini or your plants unexpectedly produced an enormous, or bumper, crop of the squash. This is why I've highlighted recipes that call for generous quantities of common types of produce with the "Bumper Crop" label, such as the following:

- **Cucumbers:** Sweetened Cucumber Relish (page 123)
- **Cabbage:** Cultured Curtido (page 100)
- **Beans:** Classic Dilly Beans (page 62)
- **Beets:** Water Bath–Processed Beets (page 65)
- **Corn:** Grilled Cherry Tomato and Corn Salsa (page 142)
- **Peppers:** Bell Pepper Slices (page 46)
- **Summer Squash:** Zucchini Relish (page 124)
- **Tomatoes:** Green Tomato Chutney (page 134)

These recipes fill standard-size canners and fermenting vessels. If your harvest is larger, simply prepare multiple batches.

Outfit Your Kitchen

Pickling can use many types of tools, but it's often possible to make do with what you already own, especially if you start with a simple quick pickle from chapter 2. It's more important to treat the equipment you use properly. Gather your tools and make sure they're in good shape, clean, and dry before you begin.

Must-Have Tools

Most essential pickling equipment is likely already in your kitchen: sharp knives, cutting boards, bowls, rubber spatulas, peelers, measuring cups and spoons, ladles, paper and cloth towels, nonreactive pots and pans, pot holders, and timers. A few other items can help. See Resources (page 194) for my preferred products.

JARS

Home-canned pickles require reusable mason jars: quarts, pints, and for some sauces, ½-pints. Jars that once held commercially processed pickles won't withstand home processing's high heat but can store quick or refrigerator pickles. Large jars, from quarts to gallons, work for fermenting; wide mouths make assembly easy. If you ferment in a crock, you'll want jars for storage.

LIDS

Canning requires a sealable lid. Flat lids—and the rings that secure them until the seal becomes airtight—are sold with canning jars and separately. Rings can be reused if in good condition but lids cannot. When fermenting, lids keep oxygen and pests out. Air lock lids, which also let carbon dioxide escape, are the most effective and are worth the investment if you catch the fermenting bug. Nonreactive storage lids, made of materials that won't interact with the acidic contents of the jar, are also worth their price. As with cookware, options include stainless steel, food-grade plastic, silicone, and unleaded glass.

CANNER

You don't need a dedicated kettle to can, but you do need one that has a rack and a lid and is tall enough to cover the jars by at least 1 inch of water without boiling over. I also recommend a jar lifter to move full jars in and out of the canner safely.

In 2015, the USDA approved steam canners. Recipes safe for a boiling-water bath can be processed in a steam canner. Follow the manufacturer's directions or federal guidelines. Cucumbers and zucchini can be pasteurized at low temperatures to improve crispness; again, see USDA guidelines for details. Save your pressure canner for low-acid foods; it would turn pickles and relishes to mush. Multicookers, even those with a canning setting, have not been approved by the USDA.

WEIGHTS

Weight choice is less important than its goal: keeping the food submerged in brine. Weight options range from a cabbage leaf or cheesecloth, to a resealable bag or jar of brine, to specialized weights. A narrow-mouth nonreactive lid fit inside a wide-mouth jar works as a light weight. If you ferment regularly, consider glass weights designed to fit standard canning jars or crocks. Repacking from wide jars into narrower tall ones can also raise brine level.

Nice-to-Have Items

Additional tools make the prep work in pickling easier. Other tools help specifically when canning or fermenting, so consider them for your wish list.

KITCHEN PREP TOOLS

I find a kitchen scale immensely useful when pickling, particularly when canning and fermenting large batches. Homegrown produce tends to vary widely in weight and size, particularly compared with market produce, and every person chops and measures an onion differently. If your volumes don't match those given in a recipe, use a scale and aim to match the weight instead.

For general food prep, a few other tools can make pickling easier and faster. A food processor can save significant time, particularly when making large batches. An immersion blender makes it easy to puree sauces, particularly hot ones. Consider a zester for citrus, a mandoline for thin slicing, a fine-mesh colander for straining, and finely woven cheesecloth for myriad uses.

CANNING TOOLS

Canning kits often include an array of tools, but the only one I keep around (besides the must-have jar lifter described with canners on page 20) is a wide-mouth funnel; it significantly reduces mess. I remove bubbles with a bamboo or wooden chopstick. I judge headspace by using the jar's thread: If you run a measuring tape from a canning jar's rim toward its bottom, you'll notice that at ½ inch, you hit the bottom end of the jar's threads on a wide-mouth jar and the collar below the threads on a narrow-mouth jar.

FERMENTING TOOLS

For a fermenting investment, consider a crock, kraut pounder, and pH meter. Modern crocks often come with specially fitted weights and a water-lock rim, making fermentation nearly foolproof. Today's crocks range from the traditional 5 and 10 liters down to 2-liter and smaller vessels. The ½-gallon recipes in chapter 4 usually fit a 2-liter crock; to use another size, scale all ingredients, including the salt. A kraut pounder is particularly useful for cabbage or chile-heavy recipes. A pH meter shows when your fermented pickles have hit pH 4.6 and are ready for storage.

THE AROMA OF FERMENTING

Fermenting creates a potent odor, both briny and sour. It intensifies as a ferment acidifies, which is desirable for preservation but may wrinkle your nose. Some foods smell more than others; potatoes off-gas heavily, as can brassicas such as cabbage and kohlrabi. Although pungent, this indicates hardworking beneficial bacteria. In contrast, a yeasty odor means that trapped oxygen has caused filmy kahm yeast to develop, and a rotting smell means spoilage. The simplest way to clamp down on fermenting aroma while also protecting produce from oxygen exposure and rancidity is to use an air lock (see "Lids," page 20).

Pickle Troubleshooting

Some less-than-perfect pickles may still be edible, as long as they are firm, sour, and free of mold. Discard any that smell spoiled, have compromised canning seals, or are moldy, mushy, slimy, or otherwise off-putting.

Overall Solutions

Most pickle problems can be solved by general good practices. Choose fresh produce, double-check for proper salt and/or vinegar, keep produce submerged, provide an ideal fermentation temperature, use an air lock or water-sealed crock, and check jar seals when canning. If you still haven't resolved the issue, try these solutions:

SYMPTOM	PROBLEM	SOLUTION	KEEP OR TOSS?
Mold	Undesirable bacteria	Use clean equipment Leave less headspace	Toss
Mushy or slimy texture	Undesirable bacteria	Follow processing time and adjustment Remove kahm yeast	Toss
Softness	Age, too little salt, heat	Distribute salt evenly Pack the vessel firmly Remove kahm yeast Expected from a boiling-water bath	Keep
Hollow center	Inadequate watering, age	Choose smaller, less mature vegetables	Keep
Discoloration	Minerals, air exposure, poor fermentation	Use distilled water Use whole spices and pure salt Use nonreactive equipment Block light Stop fermenting earlier	Keep

Canning Troubleshooting

Reread "Canning, Step by Step" (page 6) and your chosen recipe to make sure you properly prepare and process your pickles. Common missteps include overly tight or loose rings, too much or too little headspace, and air bubbles. If you still haven't resolved the issue, try these solutions:

SYMPTOM	PROBLEM	SOLUTION	KEEP OR TOSS?
Buckled lid	Overtight ring	Screw just finger-tight	Keep, but immediately refrigerate and eat
Liquid loss	Too much air, overpacking	Pack jars less tightly Leave in the canner for 5 minutes after processing	Keep if sealed
Failed seal	Poor processing, damaged equipment	Check jars for chips Wipe jar rims Use new canning lids Follow processing times and adjustment	Keep, but immediately refrigerate and eat; toss if discovered during storage

Fermenting Troubleshooting

Reread "Fermentation, Step by Step" (page 9) and your chosen recipe for best practices. These include measuring salt as listed, maintaining an ideal temperature, keeping produce submerged, and using an air lock or water-sealed crock. You can also try these solutions:

SYMPTOM	PROBLEM	SOLUTION	KEEP OR TOSS?
Yeasty surface and/or smell	Limited lactobacilli activity	Leave less headspace Remove kahm yeast as it forms	Keep
No or few bubbles	Limited lactobacilli activity	Use distilled water Release trapped air bubbles	Keep
Too many bubbles or overflow	High-sugar produce	Leave more headspace Set the vessel on a plate Skim off foam Use a thinner weight Use less produce and brine	Keep
Too salty	High pH	Let ferment longer Mix or rinse before eating	Keep
Too sour	Low pH	Stop fermenting earlier	Keep
Not enough brine	Low water content	Make more at the given concentration Add or increase weight Cut in thinner slices	Keep

Bell Pepper Slices, page 46

Quick Pickles

Sunomono (Japanese-Style Pickled Cucumbers)

Serves 4   **Prep time:** 10 minutes   **Curing time:** 10 minutes

For many Westerners, a quickly pickled cucumber salad served with sushi may be the first exposure to Japanese pickles, called *tsukemono*. One of my favorite sushi restaurants serves a *sunomono* salad that inspired this recipe. In season, I use a thinner-skinned lemon cucumber or pickling cucumber, but even a thicker-skinned slicing cucumber will work if it's sliced ultra-thin.

1 small slicing cucumber or 2 lemon or pickling cucumbers (32 slices)

1 teaspoon Diamond Crystal kosher salt, divided

3 tablespoons unseasoned rice vinegar (4.3% acidity)

2 tablespoons water

2 teaspoons sugar

1 (2-inch) piece carrot, grated (optional)

2 thin slices red onion (optional)

¼ teaspoon grated fresh ginger (optional)

½ teaspoon toasted sesame seeds

1. Using a mandoline or very sharp knife, slice the cucumber as thin as possible. Sprinkle the slices with ¼ teaspoon of salt and set aside.

2. In a small lidded container or jar, combine the remaining ¾ teaspoon of salt, rice vinegar, water, and sugar. Cap securely and shake until the salt and sugar dissolve.

3. Rinse the salt from the cucumber slices under cool water, then gently squeeze out the water. Divide the cucumber slices among four personal serving bowls. Top each serving with a pinch each of carrot, onion, and ginger (if using), then sprinkle with sesame seeds. Drizzle each portion with the vinegar brine and let sit for at least 10 minutes before serving. Leftover pickles can be stored, submerged in their brine, in the refrigerator but are best eaten within 2 to 3 days.

Ingredient Tip: Carrot, onion, and ginger enhance the flavor of this simple salad, but you need only tiny portions, almost like a garnish.

Sweet and Spicy Cucumbers

Makes 2 to 3 cups   **Prep time:** 10 minutes, plus 30 minutes salting time   **Curing time:** 30 minutes

A blend of hot sauce and maple syrup creates these pickles in a snap with just a few ingredients. They're a great way to showcase your homemade hot sauce.

1 large (12 ounces) slicing or English cucumber

3 teaspoons Diamond Crystal kosher salt, divided

½ cup white wine vinegar (5% acidity)

½ cup water

1 tablespoon maple syrup

1 teaspoon Fermented Red Hot Sauce (page 126) or bottled hot sauce

Freshly ground black pepper

1. Peel the cucumber if it has a thick or waxy skin, then cut it into bite-size cubes. In a small bowl, toss the cubes with 2 teaspoons of salt and let sit for 30 minutes.

2. In a medium measuring cup, whisk the vinegar, water, and remaining 1 teaspoon of salt until the salt dissolves. Stir in the maple syrup, hot sauce, and pepper until the ingredients combine.

3. Drain the liquid from the cucumbers, rinse them under cool water, then drain again before patting the cucumbers dry with a dish towel. Pour the brine over the cucumbers, ensuring they are submerged. Let sit for at least 30 minutes before serving. Leftover pickles can be stored in the refrigerator submerged in their brine but are best eaten within a few days.

Smashed Cucumbers

Makes about 3 cups

Prep time: 10 minutes, plus
15 to 30 minutes salting time

This Szechuan pickle, called *pai huang gua*, gets a flavor boost by whacking the cucumbers into irregular shapes that quickly absorb the brine. I like to use pickling cucumbers or, out of season, English cucumbers because they don't have the bitter skin of waxed burpless cucumbers. If you're growing your own, seeds for heirloom Asian cucumbers, which tend to be long, slender, and thin ribbed, are increasingly available.

4 pickling cucumbers or
  1 large English or Asian
  cucumber

1 teaspoon Diamond Crystal
  kosher salt

1 tablespoon unseasoned rice
  vinegar (4.3% acidity)

2 garlic cloves, minced

1 teaspoon soy sauce

½ teaspoon toasted
  sesame oil

½ teaspoon sugar

¼ teaspoon Szechuan
  peppercorns, crushed

1 teaspoon chile oil

½ teaspoon toasted
  sesame seeds

1. Cut the ends off the cucumbers. Cut each cucumber crosswise into 4- to 5-inch lengths. Place the pieces on a flat surface; for less mess, first enclose them in a large resealable bag. Using a small skillet or large cleaver, sharply whack the cucumbers until they are flattened and split lengthwise into spears. Cut the cucumber spears on the diagonal into 1- to 1½-inch pieces and transfer them to a colander set over a bowl. Toss the cucumbers with the salt and let sit for 15 to 30 minutes.

2. Meanwhile, in a small measuring cup, stir together the vinegar and garlic and let sit for at least 5 minutes, until the garlic flavor mellows. Whisk in the soy sauce, sesame oil, sugar, and peppercorns, stirring until the sugar dissolves.

3. Pat the salted cucumbers dry with a dish towel; pour out the liquid, and then transfer the cucumber pieces to the bowl. Toss with the vinegar brine. These pickles are best eaten immediately but can be refrigerated for up to 24 hours submerged in their brine. Just before serving, sprinkle with the chile oil and sesame seeds and toss to combine.

Ingredient Tip: A thicker-skinned cucumber can be partially peeled in vertical stripes, leaving some skin intact to help retain its shape when smashed. If a cucumber has large seeds, cut it in half and scoop them out with a grapefruit spoon or small knife before smashing.

Szechuan peppercorns have a sharp flavor, like black peppercorns, but with a tingly, lightly citrusy note. You can find them at Asian markets and spice shops, but freshly ground black pepper is a quick substitute.

Spring Asparagus

Makes about 4 cups   **Prep time:** 10 minutes, plus 5 minutes infusing time   **Curing time:** 1 to 2 hours

As soon as my garlic bulbs and early asparagus start to grow, out comes this recipe. Spring garlic is immature and harvested when it looks like a scallion; you can often find it in farmers' markets in early spring, and it's a great way to use clumps of garlic you might have missed in your fall harvest when they start to sprout again. Homegrown young onions or Egyptian walking onions can replace scallions.

1½ cups white wine vinegar (5% acidity)

1½ cups water

¼ cup sugar

1 teaspoon Morton pickling salt

1 teaspoon black peppercorns

1 teaspoon yellow mustard seeds

Pinch chili flakes

20 medium asparagus spears (1 pound)

2 whole spring garlic stalks or 1 garlic clove, minced

2 whole scallions

1. In a medium saucepan, bring the vinegar, water, sugar, and salt to a boil, stirring to dissolve the sugar and salt. Remove the pan from the heat and add the peppercorns, mustard seeds, and chili flakes; let infuse for 5 minutes.

2. Cut the ends of the asparagus off and cut the spring garlic and scallions to a similar length. In a clean, shallow container with a lid, arrange them evenly. Pour the brine over the vegetables, cover the container, and let sit for 1 to 2 hours before serving.

3. For longer storage, remove the garlic and scallions and strain the brine, collecting it in a large measuring cup. Pack the asparagus into two clean, tall 24-ounce jars and pour the brine over the spears, ensuring they are submerged. Screw on a nonreactive lid and store in the refrigerator, where the pickles will keep for months.

Pickled Avocado Slices

Makes 1 pint   **Prep time:** 10 minutes, plus 30 minutes cooling time   **Curing time:** 2 to 4 hours

If pickles and avocado toast appeal, you'll fall for this quick pickle. It's all about timing: Rock-hard avocados will have little flavor, but fully ripe ones will be too soft to hold their sliced shape. Plus, after 12 hours, the brine starts to overpower the mild flavor of the avocado. If you do let the pickle sit longer, mix it with a fresh ripe avocado to bring back the flavor before spreading it on toast.

½ cup white wine vinegar (5% acidity)

½ cup water

1¼ teaspoons Morton pickling salt

1 teaspoon sugar

1 garlic clove, smashed

½ teaspoon black peppercorns

½ teaspoon chile flakes

2 firm, underripe avocados

2 teaspoons chopped fresh cilantro

Zest of ½ lime

1. In a small saucepan, bring the vinegar, water, salt, and sugar to a boil, stirring to dissolve the salt and sugar. Remove the pan from the heat and add the garlic, peppercorns, and chile flakes; let the brine infuse for about 30 minutes, until it has cooled to room temperature. Fish the garlic clove out of the brine and put it in the bottom of a clean wide-mouth pint jar.

2. When the brine has cooled, peel and pit the avocados, then cut the flesh into ¼-inch-thick slices. Sprinkle the slices with cilantro and lime zest and gently pack them into the jar. Ladle in the brine, ensuring the avocado slices are submerged. Cover and refrigerate for 2 to 4 hours before eating. These pickles are best eaten within 12 hours but can be stored in the refrigerator submerged in brine and eaten within a few days.

Ingredient Tip: If the avocado skin doesn't easily pull away from the flesh, insert a soup spoon along the edge at the same angle as the flesh and scoop it out.

Try It With: Pickled avocado slices hold their shape surprisingly well, so lay them on toast, salads, or burgers. Or you can mash them—on their own or mixed with fresh avocado—before smearing them on toast and piling on your favorite toppings.

Roasted Beet Pickles

Makes 1 pint

Prep time: 10 minutes, plus 30 minutes cooling time

Beets require more work than most pickles because you have to cook them first. I like to use a couple of cooked beets left over from another meal for quick pickles so that they remain "quick." These beets can be boiled, roasted, grilled, or smoked before they go into the brine. Boiling may seem simplest, but the other cooking methods will give you more flavor.

½ cup white wine vinegar (5% acidity)

½ cup water

½ cup raw cane sugar or granulated sugar

2 teaspoons Morton pickling salt

1 teaspoon black peppercorns

4 (2-inch) strips orange peel

2 medium beets, roasted and peeled (for roasting and peeling instructions, see Water Bath–Processed Beets, page 65); (2 cups)

1. In a small saucepan, bring the vinegar, water, sugar, salt, peppercorns, and orange peel to a simmer, stirring until the sugar dissolves. Meanwhile, using a mandoline or very sharp knife, cut the cooked beets into ¼-inch or thinner slices. Add the beets to the simmering brine, remove the pan from the heat, and let sit for at least 30 minutes, until they have cooled to room temperature.

2. Strain the beets from the brine, collecting the brine in a small measuring cup. Eat immediately or pack the beets into a clean pint jar and pour in the brine, ensuring the slices are submerged. Screw on a nonreactive lid and store in the refrigerator for up to 2 weeks.

Try It With: Beets, especially red ones, are messy if eaten directly with your fingers. Slice these beets as thin as possible, and you can serve them on crackers or pita bread with cheese and fresh basil.

Orange and Golden Beets with Roasted Garlic

Makes about 2 cups   **Prep time:** 10 minutes   **Curing time:** 30 minutes

This introductory pickle recipe uses the same techniques as other quick pickles, but the sweetness of the balsamic vinegar and orange juice makes the beets less acidic. This also means they don't keep as long and are best made just before they are eaten.

1 pound small golden beets, roasted and peeled (for roasting and peeling instructions, see Water Bath–Processed Beets, page 65) (2 cups)

4 roasted garlic cloves

2 tablespoons freshly squeezed orange juice

1 tablespoon balsamic vinegar (6% acidity)

2 slices red onion, minced (1 teaspoon)

Pickling or sea salt

Freshly ground black pepper

1 tablespoon extra-virgin olive oil (optional)

1. Cut the beets into ¼-inch-thick slices and put them in a shallow bowl or container. Into a small measuring cup, squeeze the roasted garlic, then mash it with a fork. Add the orange juice, vinegar, and onion, whisking with the fork until the mixture is combined.

2. Pour the liquid over the beets, tossing gently to coat; add salt and pepper to taste. Refrigerate for at least 30 minutes. If desired, drizzle the beets with oil just before serving. These beets are best eaten within a few hours.

Ingredient Tip: A gourmet grocery store may sell roasted garlic in its antipasti section, but it's easy to roast at home. Set a whole, unpeeled head on a baking tray, drizzle it with a little olive oil, and bake at 350°F for 30 to 45 minutes, depending on the size and age of the head, until the paper around the cloves begins to brown and the cloves are slightly soft to the touch.

Eight-Hour Curtido (Cabbage Slaw)

Makes 1 quart

Prep time: 20 minutes, plus
2 hours salting time

Curing time: 6 hours

This lightly pickled cabbage slaw originates in El Salvador and offers a great twist on traditional coleslaw. Purple carrots and red onion turn the brine pink the longer it sits, but you can replace these with orange carrots and yellow or white onion for a less colorful mix. Out of season, feel free to use dried oregano instead of fresh.

¼ medium green or white cabbage, shredded (3½ cups)

2 medium purple carrots, grated (1 cup)

1 small red onion, thinly sliced (1 cup)

2 teaspoons Diamond Crystal kosher salt

1 tablespoon minced fresh oregano or 1 teaspoon crumbled dried oregano

1 serrano chile, thinly sliced (1½ tablespoons)

½ cup apple cider vinegar (5% acidity)

½ cup water

½ teaspoon brown sugar

1. In a large bowl, combine the cabbage, carrots, and onion. Sprinkle with the salt and toss to combine. Cover the bowl with a dish towel and let sit for about 2 hours, occasionally massaging the vegetables to release more liquid.

2. Uncover the bowl and sprinkle the vegetables with the oregano and chile slices before tossing to combine. Pack the vegetables loosely into a clean wide-mouth quart jar.

3. In a medium measuring cup, whisk the vinegar, water, and sugar until the sugar dissolves. Pour the brine over the vegetables, pressing them down under the liquid until they are submerged. Screw on a nonreactive lid and store in the refrigerator for at least 6 hours before eating. As long as the vegetables stay submerged, the curtido will keep for weeks in the refrigerator.

Don't Forget: Many tools, including a food processor with a slicer attachment, work for the vegetable prep, but I prefer a sharp knife for shredding cabbage, a large-holed cheese grater for grating carrots, and a mandoline for thinly slicing onions.

Carrot and Daikon Radish

Makes 2 cups　　　　**Prep time:** 10 minutes, plus 20 minutes salting time　　　　**Curing time:** 1 to 2 hours

Vietnamese meals typically include pickled carrots and daikon radish, served as a salad or condiment. You'll find this simple pickle in banh mi sandwiches or on a mixed salad plate. It's also delicious in rice-paper-wrapped summer rolls and tossed with rice noodles and fresh vegetables for a light lunch. Daikon radish, a long, thick white tuber, might be sold whole or in sections in your produce department.

2 medium carrots (1 cup)

1 (2½-inch) piece daikon radish (1 cup)

1½ teaspoons Diamond Crystal kosher salt

¼ cup unseasoned rice vinegar (4.3% acidity)

1 tablespoon sugar

¼ teaspoon minced fresh ginger

1. Using a mandoline with a fine julienne or coarse grating blade, shred the carrots and radish; alternatively, use a very sharp knife to cut the vegetables into thin matchsticks. Transfer the carrot and radish to a colander set over a bowl, toss with the salt, and let sit for 20 minutes.

2. In a small measuring cup, combine the vinegar and sugar. Stir until the sugar dissolves, then stir in the ginger.

3. Rinse the salt from the vegetables under cool water, then gently squeeze out the water. Transfer the carrot and radish to a clean lidded container, pour the brine over the vegetables, and toss to mix well. Refrigerate for 1 to 2 hours before straining and serving chilled. Leftover pickles can be stored, submerged in their brine, in the refrigerator for a couple of weeks.

Switch Things Up: You can use just carrots, just radish, or different proportions of each, depending on what you have on hand. If you don't have a mandoline, a good knife is better than a food processor, which tends to shred too finely.

Ginger-Spiked Carrot and Apple Pickle

Makes 1½ cups

Prep time: 10 minutes, plus
30 minutes salting time

This flavorful pickle resembles thinly shaved pickled ginger with a sweeter twist thanks to the natural sugars in carrots and apples. Choose a crisp apple, such as a Fuji, Braeburn, or, for extra tartness, Granny Smith. A little lemon juice or vinegar tossed onto the apple as soon as it is sliced will help slow browning during the salting phase. Try this as a tangy grated salad.

2 medium carrots (1 cup)

1 medium crisp apple,
   quartered (1 cup)

1 (2-inch) piece peeled
   fresh ginger

Splash of freshly squeezed
   lemon juice or vinegar

2 teaspoons Diamond Crystal
   kosher salt

½ cup unseasoned rice
   vinegar (4.3% acidity)

¼ cup sherry

1½ teaspoons sugar

1 tablespoon coriander
   seeds, crushed

1. Using a mandoline or very sharp knife, cut the carrots, apple quarters, and ginger crosswise into paper-thin pieces with a similar diameter. Transfer the vegetables to a colander set over a bowl, toss with the lemon juice and then the salt, and let sit for 30 minutes.

2. In a small measuring cup, combine the vinegar, sherry, and sugar. Stir until the sugar dissolves, then stir in the coriander seeds.

3. Rinse the salt from the vegetables under cool water, then gently squeeze out the water. Transfer the vegetables to a bowl, pour in the brine, and toss to mix well before serving. These pickles will keep for at least 1 week in a clean lidded container in the refrigerator submerged in their brine.

Rainbow Chard Stems

Makes 1 cup

Prep time: 10 minutes, plus
30 minutes cooling time

I first tried pickled chard on homemade sourdough pizza and have been hooked on these bright bites ever since. I like to make them with young homegrown stems before they become stringy, but by cutting them in slices you can avoid the need to remove the strings from full-grown chard. Rainbow chard pickles will be brightest if eaten straightaway.

½ cup apple cider vinegar (5% acidity)

½ cup water

2 tablespoons sugar

1 teaspoon Morton pickling salt

1 garlic clove, smashed

⅛ teaspoon fennel seeds

⅛ teaspoon celery seeds

3 rainbow chard stems, cut into ¼-inch slices (1 cup)

In a small saucepan, bring the vinegar, water, sugar, salt, and garlic to a boil, stirring to dissolve the sugar and salt. Add the fennel seeds, celery seeds, and chard stems. Simmer for 30 seconds to blanch the stems, then remove from the heat. Let sit for about 30 minutes, until cooled to room temperature. Drain and use immediately, or transfer the chard stems and brine to a clean lidded container and store submerged in their brine in the refrigerator for up to a week.

Try It With: Besides pizza, pickled rainbow chard is delicious in sushi rolls, as a relish with grilled halibut or snapper, or tossed in a mixed bean or cabbage salad.

Corn and Chile Pickle

Makes 2 (12-ounce) jars   **Prep time:** 10 minutes   **Curing time:** 30 minutes

Pickled corn is often categorized as a salsa or relish, but I always think of this old-fashioned recipe as a pickle because it is more acidic than fresh salsa and isn't cooked like a canned relish. Still, the size of the corn kernels means you won't likely eat it as finger food. Instead, try it as a bruschetta topping or as a garnish for crudo. Or defy classification and just dig in with tortilla chips.

1½ cups corn kernels (cut from 2 ears)

1 medium onion, minced (½ cup)

1 Anaheim pepper or other mild chile, minced (¼ cup)

1 jalapeño pepper or serrano chile, minced (1½ tablespoons)

½ teaspoon coriander seeds, crushed

¼ teaspoon yellow mustard seeds, crushed

½ cup white wine vinegar (5% acidity)

½ cup water

¼ cup bottled lime juice (5% acidity)

1 teaspoon Diamond Crystal kosher salt

1. In a medium bowl, combine the corn, onion, peppers, and coriander and mustard seeds, and toss to mix. Divide the vegetables between two clean 12-ounce jars.

2. In a small measuring cup, combine the vinegar, water, lime juice, and salt. Stir until the salt dissolves. Pour the brine over the vegetables in each jar, ensuring they are submerged. Screw a nonreactive lid on each and let sit for at least 30 minutes before eating. For longer storage, refrigerate submerged in brine for up to 1 month.

Russian-Inspired Pickled Mushrooms

Makes 1 pint **Prep time:** 15 minutes **Curing time:** 2 hours

I ate many pickled wild mushrooms when I lived in Russia, usually boiled and stored in vinegar and oil. But I failed to replicate their meaty texture until I learned about mushroom denaturation. By marinating raw mushrooms in vinegar, you essentially "cook" them. This recipe works with many types of mushroom, including chestnut boletes, king oysters, blue oysters, and the humble cremini.

8 ounces mushrooms (2½ cups)

¼ cup white wine vinegar (5% acidity)

¼ cup boiling water

1 teaspoon Morton pickling salt

1 teaspoon sugar

1 teaspoon Sweet-Savory Spice Blend (page 16)

1 bay leaf

¼ teaspoon dill seeds

1 tablespoon extra-virgin olive oil, for serving (optional)

1. Cut the mushrooms into slices or pieces less than 1¼ inch in diameter and put them in a clean lidded container. In a small measuring cup, whisk together the vinegar, boiling water, salt, and sugar, stirring until the salt and sugar dissolve. Pour the brine over the mushrooms, then add the spice blend, bay leaf, and dill seeds; stir to combine. Let sit at room temperature for 2 hours, stirring occasionally so that all the mushrooms are exposed to the brine.

2. To serve, strain the mushrooms, tossing them with olive oil, if desired. Leftover mushrooms can be stored in the refrigerator submerged in their brine, without oil; the brine should cover the mushrooms now that they've released their liquid. They are best eaten within 2 weeks.

Ingredient Tip: Wild and substrate-cultivated mushrooms can hold dirt or sawdust. If brushing them with a dry or damp cloth doesn't remove these particles, drop them in a bowl of cold salted water, agitate them briefly, drain them through a colander, and let them dry completely on a dish towel.

Mushrooms Pickled in White Wine

Makes 1 pint   **Prep time:** 15 minutes   **Curing time:** 2 hours at room temperature, plus 1 hour refrigerated

When my mom shared a wine-pickled mushroom recipe from her 1978 edition of *The Picnic Gourmet*, I liked the idea but not the recipe. So I built one on its concept. These mushrooms become pickled as they denature in wine. The recipe is particularly delicious if you use the caps of chestnut bolete mushrooms or king oysters, cut lengthwise down their caps and stems into ½-inch sticks, but small cremini mushrooms also work well.

8 ounces mushroom caps and/or slices (2½ cups)

¼ medium onion, finely chopped (2 tablespoons)

¼ cup white wine, such as sauvignon blanc or pinot grigio

¼ cup boiling water

1 tablespoon white wine vinegar (5% acidity)

1 teaspoon Morton pickling salt

1 tablespoon finely chopped fresh dill or 1 teaspoon dried dill

1 teaspoon black peppercorns, crushed

½ teaspoon prepared stone-ground mustard or German-Inspired Spicy Mustard (page 151)

2 tablespoons extra-virgin olive oil, for serving

1. In a clean lidded container, combine the mushrooms and onion. In a small measuring cup, whisk together the wine, boiling water, vinegar, and salt, stirring until the salt dissolves. Pour the liquid over the mushrooms, tossing to combine. Let sit at room temperature for 2 hours, stirring occasionally, so that all the mushrooms are exposed to the liquid.

2. Stir the dill, peppercorns, and mustard into the mushrooms and refrigerate them for at least 1 hour, until completely chilled, and up to 24 hours before serving. To serve, strain most of the liquid from the mushrooms and toss them with the olive oil; eat immediately. Leftover mushrooms can be stored in the refrigerator submerged in their brine, without oil; they are best eaten within 2 weeks.

Red Onions in Wine Vinegar

Makes 2 cups   **Prep time:** 10 minutes, plus 20 minutes salting time   **Cook time:** 5 minutes
Curing time: 1 hour

Red onions are fun to pickle in vinegar, because they quickly turn the brine bright pink. Using red wine vinegar gives them an even faster color boost. I cut these onions fairly thick and layer them between homemade sourdough brioche buns and black bean veggie burgers. The hint of mustard flavor comes through more strongly when I smear the buns with German-Inspired Spicy Mustard (page 151).

1 medium red onion, cut into ¼- to ½-inch-thick rings (1¾ cups)

1½ teaspoons Diamond Crystal kosher salt

½ cup red wine vinegar (5% acidity)

½ cup water

1 tablespoon sugar

1 bay leaf

1 garlic clove, smashed

1 teaspoon black peppercorns

1 teaspoon yellow mustard seeds

½ teaspoon brown mustard seeds

1. Put the onion in a colander set over a medium heatproof bowl, toss with the salt, and let sit for 20 minutes.

2. Gently squeeze the onion with your hands. Discard the collected liquid, wipe the bowl dry, and transfer the drained onion to the bowl. Set the colander back over the bowl and line it with cheesecloth.

3. In a small saucepan, bring the vinegar, water, sugar, bay leaf, garlic, peppercorns, and mustard seeds to a boil, stirring occasionally to dissolve the sugar. Lower the heat so that the liquid simmers for about 3 minutes, until the flavors infuse the vinegar. Strain the hot brine through the colander and over the onions, discarding the solids in the compost. Let sit for at least 1 hour, stirring occasionally, until cooled to room temperature and uniformly pink.

4. To eat, remove the onions with a slotted spoon and let them drain completely. Leftover pickles can be packed in a clean lidded container, submerged in their brine, and stored in the refrigerator; they are best eaten within 1 week.

Lime-Pickled Onions

Makes 2 cups   **Prep time:** 10 minutes, plus   **Curing time:** 3 hours
                          30 minutes salting time

When I traveled in Ecuador, traditional meals were often accompanied by a spicy onion pickle infused with lime flavor. I learned that they were made by simply letting the raw onions stew in lime juice. A few tricks and salt bring out the flavor while reducing the sharpness of the onion and lime. I love them on baked potatoes or on homemade sourdough bagels with Gravlax (page 178).

1 medium red onion, cut into paper-thin rings (1¾ cups)

1 tablespoon Diamond Crystal kosher salt

Zest of 1 lime

Juice of 2 limes or ¼ cup bottled lime juice (5% acidity)

1. In a clean lidded container, toss the onion with the salt, and let sit for about 20 minutes. Toss the onion again, cover with room-temperature water, and let sit for another 10 minutes.

2. Transfer the onion to a colander. Rinse away the salt under cool water, then drain completely. Return the drained onion to the container. Add the lime zest and juice and mix well.

3. Cover the onions and store in the refrigerator for at least 3 hours, stirring occasionally to ensure they turn uniformly pink. The pickles will keep for several days submerged in brine and stored in the refrigerator.

Ingredient Tip: Several tricks release the most juice from a lime or lemon. Make sure it's at room temperature. Roll it back and forth, pressing gently a few times before cutting it lengthwise. Press the tines of a fork deeply into each half, rotating the fork as you squeeze.

Minty Snap Peas

Makes 1 quart

Prep time: 20 minutes, plus 40 minutes cooling time

Curing time: 24 hours

No matter how much effort I put into staggering pea planting in my garden, my cool, long-day climate inevitably sets all the pods at once. Still, snap peas taste best fresh from the vine. At room temperature, half their sugars turn to starch within 6 hours. But if you quickly pickle your harvest, you can capture some of that sweetness with the tang of vinegar.

1 cup unseasoned rice vinegar (4.3% acidity)

¾ cup water

Juice of 1 lemon or 3 tablespoons bottled lemon juice (5% acidity)

1 tablespoon sugar

½ teaspoon Morton pickling salt

¼ teaspoon aniseed (optional)

4 mint sprigs, divided

Zest of 1 lemon

1 pound sugar snap peas, strings removed

1. In a small saucepan, bring the vinegar, water, lemon juice, sugar, and salt to a simmer, stirring to dissolve the salt and sugar. Remove the pan from the heat and add the aniseed (if using) and 2 mint sprigs; let the brine infuse for about 10 minutes, until cool enough to handle.

2. Meanwhile, in the bottom of a warm, clean wide-mouth quart jar, sprinkle the lemon zest, and then tip the jar at a 45-degree angle. Add the remaining 2 mint sprigs down one side. Pack the sugar snap peas into the jar, layering them so that they hold the mint in and will be vertical when you set the jar upright.

3. Set a fine-mesh colander over a medium measuring cup, lining it with cheesecloth if the holes are large enough to let the seeds slip through. Strain the warm brine through the colander, discarding the solids in the compost. Pour the brine into the jar, ensuring the peas are submerged. Cover loosely with a nonreactive lid and let sit for 30 minutes or until completely cooled. Tighten the lid and store in the refrigerator for at least 24 hours before eating. The pickles are best eaten in a couple of weeks but will keep for months submerged in their brine in the refrigerator.

Ingredient Tip: Aniseed has a strong licorice flavor, so keeping the seeds out of the jar prevents them from overpowering the brine. For a milder flavor, substitute fennel seeds. If you find the mint to be too strong after a couple of weeks, it can be pulled out as well.

Chile Rings

Makes 1 pint **Prep time:** 10 minutes, plus 30 minutes cooling time **Curing time:** 30 minutes

They may seem like a fancy condiment, but pickled chile rings are simple to make and hugely versatile, both in their heat level and their uses. I prefer the smokier taste of Fresno chiles to the more ubiquitous jalapeño, but you can go hotter or milder by swapping out the type of chile. Just be sure to put on rubber gloves before you clean and slice.

1 cup apple cider vinegar (5% acidity)

¼ cup water

2 tablespoons honey

1 teaspoon Morton pickling salt

1 garlic clove, smashed

6 Fresno chiles, sliced into ¼-inch rings (1 cup)

1. In a small saucepan, heat the vinegar, water, honey, and salt over low heat, stirring, just until the honey dissolves. Remove the pan from the heat and add the garlic; let the brine infuse for about 30 minutes, until it has cooled to room temperature.

2. Fish the garlic clove out of the brine and put it in the bottom of a clean wide-mouth pint jar, then pack the chile rings into the jar. Ladle the brine over the chiles, ensuring they are submerged. Let sit at room temperature for 30 minutes before using; otherwise, screw on a nonreactive lid and store in the refrigerator submerged in their brine. The chiles hold more heat the first couple of days but will keep for weeks.

Try It With: These pickles work well with any meal, from breakfast eggs to lunchtime nachos to pad thai at dinner. Use both the pepper rings and the chile-infused vinegar they create.

Bell Pepper Slices

Makes 4 pints **Prep time:** 10 minutes, plus 30 minutes cooling time **Curing time:** 2 hours

BUMPER CROP

These pickles work well for a larger batch of freshly harvested sweet peppers. For the most colorful jars, pack blends of red, yellow, orange, and green slices. If you plan to eat the peppers after a couple of hours, you can add more colors, such as purple and brown—but these more unusual bell pepper varieties will revert to green the longer they sit in the brine, just like they do when cooked.

2 cups white wine vinegar (5% acidity)

2 cups water

¼ cup sugar

2½ teaspoons Morton pickling salt

4 or 5 large bell peppers (2 pounds), cut into strips (6 cups)

8 garlic cloves, minced

½ cup minced fresh oregano or 3 tablespoons crumbled dried oregano

1. In a medium saucepan, bring the vinegar, water, sugar, and salt to a simmer, stirring to dissolve the sugar and salt. Remove the pan from the heat and let sit for about 30 minutes, until the brine has cooled to room temperature.

2. In a medium bowl, toss the pepper strips with the garlic and oregano and divide them among four clean wide-mouth pint jars, packing them in gently.

3. Ladle the brine over the peppers, ensuring they are submerged. Screw a nonreactive lid on each jar and let sit for at least 2 hours before eating. For longer storage, refrigerate submerged in brine for weeks.

Ingredient Tip: Bell pepper slices fit vertically into wide-mouth pint jars almost perfectly, so I tend to pack them in more smaller jars rather than fewer quarts. The pints make excellent gifts. Just be sure your recipients know they haven't been canned and need to be kept in the refrigerator.

Miso Asazuke (Quick Miso Pickle)

Makes 1 cup

Prep time: 10 minutes, plus 1 hour salting time

Curing time: 24 hours

I'd heard about miso pickles long before I attempted to make them, but my first batch had me hooked. Miso pickles rely on a pickling "bed" made of miso paste and perhaps sake and sugar. No other style of pickle matches their umami flavor, which is at once sweet and sour, salty and savory. This *asazuke*, or quick, version with daikon radish can be eaten in just 24 hours.

1 (3-inch) piece daikon radish, peeled and cut into ¼-inch-thick half-moons (1 cup)

½ teaspoon Diamond Crystal kosher salt

2 tablespoons red miso

1 tablespoon sake or water

½ teaspoon sugar

Toasted sesame seeds, for garnish

1. Put the radish pieces in a colander set over a bowl, toss with the salt, and let drain for 1 hour. Rinse, drain again, and pat dry with a dish towel.

2. In a clean lidded container, mix together the miso, sake, and sugar. Add the radish slices and mix again to coat the slices and evenly distribute the miso. Store the container in the refrigerator for at least 24 hours and up to 3 days.

3. To serve, remove the radish slices, squeezing them slightly to remove excess moisture and miso; if they still seem too salty, rinse off the remaining miso under cool running water and pat the radishes dry. Garnish with toasted sesame seeds. Leftover pickles can be stored in the refrigerator but are best eaten within a few days.

Ingredient Tip: Red miso has a higher percentage of salt than white miso, so it both adds a bold flavor and speeds up the pickling process. Once you remove the radish slices, the miso can be used as a marinade for grilled shrimp.

Tangy Radish Rounds

Makes 1 cup

Prep time: 10 minutes, plus 10 minutes salting time

Radishes make a delicious quick pickle with any type of vinegar, but you can give your spring crop a flavor boost when chives begin to flower. Instead of basic white wine vinegar, swap in the strained chive-infused vinegar from the Pickled Chive Blossoms. For extra tang, use the vinegar as soon as it's ready and break apart some chive blossoms to sprinkle on the radish pickles before serving.

12 salad radishes, cut into thin rounds (1 cup)

¼ teaspoon Diamond Crystal kosher salt

2 tablespoons minced chives

1 teaspoon toasted cumin seeds, crushed

1 tablespoon peeled, grated fresh ginger

2 tablespoons white wine vinegar (5% acidity) or brine from Pickled Chive Blossoms (page 68)

1. In a small bowl, toss the radishes with the salt and let sit for 10 minutes.

2. Drain the radishes and pat them dry with a dish towel. In the bowl with the radishes, add the chives, cumin seeds, and ginger; toss to combine. Pour in the vinegar and toss again before serving immediately. Leftover radishes can be stored submerged in their brine in the refrigerator but are best eaten in 2 to 3 days.

Ingredient Tip: Cumin seeds can be toasted in a dry skillet for about 3 minutes; watch closely and stir constantly to prevent burning. Ginger is easy to peel using the edge of a small spoon and to grate using a ginger grater or zester.

Ripe Cherry Tomato Pickles

Makes 2 cups   **Prep time:** 15 minutes   **Curing time:** 1 hour

Unripened green tomatoes make fabulous pickles, but ripe red ones present challenges because they're already so soft and juicy. By choosing small cherry tomatoes, particularly if you grow a thicker-skinned heirloom variety, and pickling them briefly, you can overcome the ripe tomato's tendency to become mushy.

8 ounces heirloom Black Cherry or other cherry tomatoes (2 cups)

1 garlic clove, thinly sliced

3 tablespoons minced fresh basil

1 tablespoon minced fresh flat-leaf parsley

½ teaspoon minced fresh oregano

Freshly ground black pepper

½ cup white wine vinegar (5% acidity)

½ cup water

2 teaspoons balsamic vinegar (6% acidity)

1 teaspoon Diamond Crystal kosher salt

1. Using a sharp knife, poke a couple of holes into each tomato before placing it in a medium bowl. Add the garlic, basil, parsley, oregano, and pepper to taste and toss gently.

2. In a small measuring cup, whisk together the white wine vinegar, water, balsamic vinegar, and salt, stirring until the salt dissolves. Pour the brine over the tomatoes, ensuring they are submerged. Let sit for 1 hour, stirring occasionally to keep the tomatoes rotating in the brine before serving. Leftover pickles can be packed in a clean lidded container, submerged in their brine, and stored in the refrigerator and are best eaten within 2 weeks.

Try It With: These tomatoes are tasty on an antipasto tray with homemade feta but can also be sliced and used as a bruschetta topping. For an extra garlic kick, cut off the end of a fresh clove and rub it over the toasted bread before adding the tomatoes.

Salt-and-Vinegar Winter Squash

Makes 1 quart **Prep time:** 15 minutes, plus 2 to 4 hours salting and 30 minutes cooling time **Curing time:** 24 hours

I rarely think of pickling winter squash because it keeps so long and so well in a cool, dry space. But it makes a delicious, unusual pickle that stands out on a wintertime antipasto tray. Salting does the best job of softening the squash. The crisp, thin slices remind me of salt-and-vinegar potato chips.

1 medium (1½-pounds) butternut squash, peeled and cut into ⅛-inch-thick rounds (2¾ cups)

1 small onion, thinly sliced (1 cup)

6 teaspoons Morton pickling salt, divided

Ice cubes

12 dried pequín chiles, crushed

1 tablespoon minced fresh sage or 1 teaspoon crumbled dried sage

6 garlic cloves, smashed

1 cup apple cider vinegar (5% acidity)

1 cup water

2 teaspoons sugar

1. In a large bowl, toss the squash and onion slices with 4 teaspoons of the salt. Cover with ice cubes and let sit at room temperature for 2 to 4 hours, until the salt penetrates and softens the squash.

2. Transfer the squash and onions to a colander to drain; rinse them under cool running water, then drain again. Toss with the chiles and sage, then layer the squash and onion mixture, along with the garlic, in a clean wide-mouth quart jar.

3. In a small saucepan, bring the vinegar, water, sugar, and remaining 2 teaspoons of salt to a boil, stirring to dissolve the sugar and salt. Ladle the hot brine over the squash, ensuring it is submerged. Remove any air bubbles with a bamboo or wooden chopstick. Cover loosely with a nonreactive lid and let sit until completely cooled, about 30 minutes. Tighten the lid and store in the refrigerator for 24 hours before eating. The pickles will keep for up to 2 weeks submerged in brine in the refrigerator.

Switch Things Up: A friend grows tiny pequín chiles in her Austin, Texas, yard and brings them to me every year. If you don't have a pequín source, substitute any other dried chile; you'll likely need only 2 larger chiles.

Zucchini Escabeche (Grilled and Pickled Zucchini)

Serves 4 to 6   **Prep time:** 15 minutes   **Cook time:** 2 minutes
                                                              Curing time: 10 minutes

Escabeche is a Spanish technique that cooks food in hot oil and then douses it with a vinegar-based brine. It's mostly known as a treatment for meats, such as Escabeche-Style Fish (page 180). But it works equally well for firm vegetables, such as summer squash. By cooling the zucchini in a vinegar brine, the flavor quickly penetrates the hot squash. This cell-deep acidity helps preserve the zucchini in the refrigerator.

4 medium zucchini
(1½ pounds)

3 tablespoons extra-virgin
olive oil, divided

½ cup apple cider vinegar
(5% acidity)

1 tablespoon brown sugar

½ teaspoon Diamond Crystal
kosher salt

¾ teaspoon fresh lemon
thyme or ¼ teaspoon dried
lemon thyme

1. Cut the zucchini lengthwise into ¼-inch-thick slices and drizzle with 1 tablespoon of oil.

2. In a small measuring cup, whisk together the vinegar, the remaining 2 tablespoons of oil, the sugar, salt, and lemon thyme, stirring until the sugar and salt dissolve.

3. Cook the zucchini on a very hot grill for about 1 minute per side, or just until grill marks start to show. Alternatively, fry in a sauté pan or skillet over medium-high heat for about 1 minute per side, or just until the slices begin to brown.

4. Transfer the zucchini to a heatproof dish and immediately pour the brine over the slices. Let sit for at least 10 minutes, until the brine cools to room temperature. Serve immediately or transfer the zucchini to a clean lidded container and store submerged in its brine in the refrigerator for up to 1 month.

Ingredient Tip: The olive oil will solidify in the refrigerator, so don't be alarmed when you pull out the container. Simply let it come to room temperature or heat the zucchini slightly before serving. Lemon thyme adds a pleasant citrus note, but English thyme, the type typically sold as dried thyme, or French thyme works, too.

Personal Zucchini Pickle

Serves 1   **Prep time:** 5 minutes   **Curing time:** 15 minutes

Satisfy your pickle craving with a batch so small that you have an excuse *not* to share. It's easy to whip up for a secret snack or to go with a solo meal. It's also adaptable to almost any fruit or vegetable. The trick is to cut the produce as thin as possible and use salt to pull out its natural water so that it quickly absorbs the brine.

½ small zucchini, thinly sliced (16 slices)

2 thin slices onion

¼ teaspoon Diamond Crystal kosher salt

2 tablespoons apple cider or white wine vinegar (5% acidity)

2 tablespoons hot water

¼ teaspoon sugar (optional)

¼ teaspoon minced fresh ginger

1. Sprinkle the zucchini and onion slices with salt and set aside in a small bowl.

2. In a small lidded container or jar, combine the vinegar, hot water, and sugar (if using). Cap securely and shake until the sugar dissolves, then stir in the ginger. Drain any liquid from the vegetables, then pour the vinegar mixture over them, ensuring they are submerged, and let them sit for at least 15 minutes. Leftover pickles can be stored, submerged in their brine, in the refrigerator and are best eaten within 2 to 3 days.

Switch Things Up: Zucchini is just one personal pickle option. Try thin slices of yellow summer squash, cucumber, salad radish, carrot, or sweet pepper. Herbs and spices can be mixed into the brine to taste.

Curried Green Tomatoes, page 79

Fresh Pickles

Kosher-Style Dill Pickles

Makes 7 quarts **Prep time:** 20 minutes, plus 8 hours salting time **Processing time:** 15 minutes **Curing time:** 2 weeks

CAN THIS   **BUMPER CROP**

For a classic American pickle, look no further than dills. Always choose fresh pickling cucumbers for this recipe, preferably ones that were picked the day you put them in salt brine. Large, dark green, thick-skinned slicing cucumbers are too watery to process. Although these aren't true kosher pickles, since they move from the salt brine to a vinegar one, they do have the garlic and dill that define the NYC style.

9 pounds (4-inch or smaller) pickling cucumbers

1¼ cups Morton pickling salt, divided

2½ gallons water, divided

6 cups apple cider vinegar (5% acidity)

2 tablespoons sugar

14 slices peeled horseradish root

14 garlic cloves

7 tablespoons Basic Dilly Spice Blend (page 16)

1. Cut a thin slice from the blossom end of each cucumber (see Tip). Cut the cucumbers into spears.

2. In a large bowl, dissolve ¾ cup of salt by stirring it into 2 gallons of water. Add the cucumbers, cover the bowl with a dish towel, and let the cucumbers sit in the salt brine overnight.

3. Drain the cucumbers, rinse them under cool running water, then drain again. In a stockpot, combine the vinegar, the remaining 8 cups of water, the remaining ½ cup of salt, and the sugar. Bring the mixture to a boil, stirring to dissolve the salt and sugar. Lower the heat to just below a simmer and keep the brine hot.

4. Place 2 horseradish slices, 2 garlic cloves, and 1 tablespoon of spice blend in the bottom of each of seven clean, hot wide-mouth quart jars. Fill each jar with the cucumbers, packing them firmly but without bruising.

5. Ladle in the hot brine, submerging the cucumbers; leave ½ inch of headspace. Remove any air bubbles with a bamboo or wooden chopstick and wipe each jar's rim. Cap each jar with a two-piece canning lid. Add the jars to a boiling-water bath.

6. Process the jars in the boiling-water bath for 15 minutes, plus your altitude adjustment (see page 191). Store the jars in a dry, dark, cool place for at least 2 weeks before eating. The pickles are best eaten within a year.

Ingredient Tip: Cutting the blossom end off cucumbers removes enzymes that can make them mushy. If you can't tell the stem end and blossom end apart, slice off both. For the crispest pickles, use just-picked pickling cucumbers; you can also add horseradish or grape leaves (see "Varieties for Pickling," page 15).

Switch Things Up: For even more flavorful pickles, use the same amount of Ultra Pickling Spice Blend (page 16) or replace the dry spices with 1 fresh dill head, 1 chile, 1 bay leaf, and 1 teaspoon of mustard seeds per jar.

Honeyed Bread-and-Butter Chips

Makes 7 pints

Prep time: 20 minutes, plus 2 hours salting time

Processing time: 10 minutes
Curing time: 2 weeks

CAN THIS **BUMPER CROP**

Bread-and-butter pickles lack the cloying sweetness of sweet pickles, but the classic recipe still piles on the sugar. Swapping in honey gives more complexity and fewer grams of sugar per bite. Slice the cucumber and onion as thin as you like, but thinner slices will soften more than thick ones in a boiling-water bath.

4½ pounds (4- to 6-inch) pickling cucumbers (10 cups)

6 medium yellow onions (1½ pounds) (3 cups)

⅓ cup Morton pickling salt

2¼ cups apple cider vinegar (5% acidity)

2¼ cups water

1¼ cups honey

4½ teaspoons Bread-and-Butter Spice Blend (page 17)

4 garlic cloves, minced

1. Cut a thin slice off the blossom end of each cucumber (see Tip, page 57). Using a mandoline or very sharp knife, cut the cucumbers and onions into ¼-inch-thick rings.

2. In a large bowl, combine the cucumbers and onions, layering with the salt. Cover with ice cubes and a dish towel and let sit at room temperature for 2 hours.

3. Pour the cucumbers and onions into a colander to drain; rinse them under cool running water, then drain again. In a stockpot, combine the vinegar, water, honey, pickling spices, and garlic. Bring the mixture to a boil, stirring to dissolve the honey. Add the vegetables to the stockpot, then return the mixture to a boil.

4. Use a slotted spoon to transfer the hot slices into seven clean, hot wide-mouth pint jars, then ladle in the brine, submerging the pickles; leave ½ inch of headspace. Remove any air bubbles with a bamboo chopstick and wipe each jar's rim. Cap the jars with two-piece canning lids.

5. Process the jars in a boiling-water bath for 10 minutes, plus your altitude adjustment (see page 191). Store the jars in a dry, dark, cool place for at least 2 weeks before eating. The pickles are best eaten within a year.

Don't Forget: If this is your first time canning pickles, review the boiling-water-bath process in "Canning, Step by Step" (page 6) and the tools used here in "Outfit Your Kitchen" (page 19).

Ingredient Tip: A mandoline makes quick work of multiple batches, giving you thin, even slices. You can harvest one day and process the pickles the next if you put the ice bath in the refrigerator overnight.

Szechuan-Spiced Cucumber Rounds

Makes 1 quart

Prep time: 15 minutes, plus 2 hours salting and cooling time

Curing time: 1 week

The easiest way to keep cucumber pickles crisp is never to heat them to canning temperatures. Even so, tricks used to keep processed pickles crisp are helpful, including removing the blossom ends, salting, and chilling. Even though home gardeners may want to turn a bumper crop into shelf-stable pickles, small harvests work well as refrigerator pickles.

8 (4- to 6-inch) pickling cucumbers

1 small onion

1½ tablespoons Morton pickling salt, divided

Ice cubes

⅔ cup white wine vinegar (5% acidity)

⅔ cup water

2 teaspoons sugar

1 serrano chile, halved

4 garlic cloves, minced

12 Szechuan peppercorns

2 teaspoons toasted sesame seeds

1. Cut a thin slice off the blossom end of each cucumber (see Tip, page 57). Using a mandoline or very sharp knife, cut the onion into paper-thin rings and the cucumber into ¼-inch-thick slices, cutting the cucumbers at a slight angle.

2. In a small bowl, toss the vegetables with 4 teaspoons of salt. Cover with ice cubes and a dish towel and let sit at room temperature for 2 hours.

3. Meanwhile, in a small saucepan, bring the remaining ½ teaspoon of salt, the vinegar, water, and sugar to a simmer, stirring to dissolve the salt and sugar. Remove the pan from the heat and let sit for about 30 minutes, until the brine has cooled to room temperature. Shift the cucumbers and onions into a colander to drain; rinse them under cool running water, then drain again.

4. In the bottom of a clean, wide-mouth quart jar, combine the chile, garlic, peppercorns, and sesame seeds. Add the cucumbers, layering them with onions. Ladle the brine over the cucumbers so that they are submerged but leave ½ inch headspace. Screw on a nonreactive lid and store in the refrigerator for 1 week before eating. The pickles will keep for weeks in the refrigerator.

Cucumber Pickles with Lemon

Makes 7 pints

Prep time: 20 minutes, plus 2 hours salting time
Cook time: 5 minutes

Processing time: 10 minutes
Curing time: 2 weeks

CAN THIS **BUMPER CROP**

Some people find pickles overpowering and may be drawn to the milder tang of this recipe. Replacing some of the vinegar with lemon juice, and adding a little sweetness, gives these pickles less bite while ensuring food safety.

4½ pounds (4- to 6-inch) pickling cucumbers

1 medium red bell pepper

Ice cubes

¼ cup Morton pickling salt

4 cups white wine vinegar (5% acidity)

2¼ cups bottled lemon juice (5% acidity)

½ cup sugar

1 lemon, sliced into rounds

7 garlic cloves

7 bay leaves

3½ teaspoons black peppercorns

1. Cut a thin slice off the blossom end of each cucumber (see Tip, page 57). Using a mandoline or very sharp knife, cut the cucumbers into ¼-inch-thick rounds and the bell pepper into thin slices.

2. In a large bowl, combine the cucumbers and bell pepper, layering with the salt. Cover with ice cubes and a dish towel and let sit at room temperature for 2 hours.

3. Transfer the cucumbers and pepper to a colander to drain; rinse them under cool running water, then drain again.

4. In a stockpot, combine the vinegar, lemon juice, and sugar. Bring the mixture to a boil, stirring to dissolve the sugar. Add the cucumbers and bell peppers to the pot and return the mixture to a full boil.

5. In the bottom of each of seven clean, hot wide-mouth pint jars, place a lemon slice, garlic clove, bay leaf, and ½ teaspoon of peppercorns. Use a slotted spoon to transfer the hot vegetables into the jars, then ladle in the hot brine, submerging the pickles; leave ½ inch of headspace. Remove any air bubbles with a bamboo or wooden chopstick and wipe each jar's rim. Cap the jars with two-piece canning lids.

6. Process the pints in a boiling-water bath for 10 minutes, plus your altitude adjustment (see page 191). Store the jars in a dry, dark, cool place for at least 2 weeks before eating. The pickles are best eaten within a year.

Switch Things Up: This recipe fills a standard canner. For a smaller batch, simply halve the recipe. You can even skip the processing and refrigerate the jars instead. Let the jarred pickles cool to room temperature before moving them to the refrigerator, where they will keep for weeks.

Refrigerated Asparagus Spears

Makes 1 (24-ounce) jar

Prep time: 15 minutes, plus 30 minutes cooling time

Curing time: 3 days

CAN THIS

My large asparagus bed rarely produces enough spears in one day to bother with processing. But if you have a bumper crop of asparagus, this recipe is safe for canning, and wide-mouth 24-ounce canning jars are available. You can also cut shorter spears and divide them among 12-ounce jars, which are great for gifting.

1 teaspoon Basic Dilly Spice Blend (page 16)

15 small asparagus spears (8 ounces)

1 garlic scape or garlic clove

1 lemon slice

¾ cup white wine vinegar (at least 5% acidity)

¾ cup water

1 tablespoon sugar

½ teaspoon Morton pickling salt

1. Place the spice blend in a clean, tall 24-ounce jar. Cut the asparagus spears so that they are about ¾ inch shorter than the jar rim, then tightly pack them into the jar. Slide the garlic scape, cut to the same length as the asparagus, or garlic clove, and the lemon slice into the jar as you pack the spears.

2. In a small saucepan, bring the vinegar, water, sugar, and salt to a boil, stirring to dissolve the salt and sugar. Ladle the hot brine over the asparagus, entirely covering the spears but leaving the brine about ½ inch from the jar's rim; set aside any remaining brine. Fold a paper towel into a square that covers the jar opening and lay it over the asparagus to keep the tips submerged. Leave the jar at room temperature for 30 minutes or until completely cool.

3. When cooled, remove the paper towel and top off the jar with remaining brine as needed, or undiluted vinegar if you run out of brine, to keep the asparagus submerged. Screw on a nonreactive lid and store in the refrigerator for at least 3 days before eating. The pickles will keep for months.

Switch Things Up: To can this recipe in a boiling-water bath, multiply it by the number of 24-ounce jars you want. After filling the jars (don't place a paper towel in the jar), wipe each jar's rim, cap the jars with two-piece canning lids, and process for 15 minutes, plus your altitude adjustment (see page 191).

Classic Dilly Beans

Makes 7 pints

Prep time: 30 minutes
Processing time: 5 minutes

Curing time: 2 weeks

CAN THIS   **BUMPER CROP**

Dilly beans became popular among the cocktail crowd in the 1960s and have been a beverage garnish and snacking favorite ever since. Little has changed in the recipe over the years, and home canners have adopted it as their own. Fresh beans and dill heads are key to the crisp, dilly flavor. These annuals both grow easily from seed. If you aren't growing your own, check at your farmers' market during pickling season.

3½ pounds green and/or
  yellow snap beans (14 cups)

5 cups apple cider vinegar
  (5% acidity)

5 cups water

¼ cup Morton pickling salt

3½ teaspoons black
  peppercorns, divided

7 garlic cloves

7 dried chiles de árbol or
  other hot chiles

7 fresh dill heads

1. Snap off the bean ends, then snap each bean so that it is no more than 4 inches long, reserving any smaller pieces for fresh eating. Clean and sanitize seven wide-mouth pint jars (see "Canning, Step by Step," page 6). In a large saucepan, bring the vinegar, water, and salt just to a boil, stirring to dissolve the salt.

2. Grab one hot jar at a time with a pot holder and hold it at a 45-degree angle. Put ½ teaspoon of peppercorns, 1 garlic clove, 1 chile, and 1 dill head in each jar. Pack in the beans so that they will be vertical when you set the jars upright. Repeat

3. Ladle in the hot brine, submerging the beans; leave ½ inch of headspace. If any beans stick up into the headspace, snap off the top ends until they are submerged in the brine. Wipe the rim and cap each jar with a two-piece canning lid. Add the jars to a boiling-water bath.

4. Process the pints in the boiling-water bath for 5 minutes, plus your altitude adjustment (see page 191). Store the jars in a dry, dark, cool place for at least 2 weeks before eating. The pickles are best eaten within a year.

Szechuan-Peppered Snap Beans

Makes 7 pints   **Prep time:** 30 minutes   **Curing time:** 2 weeks
Processing time: 5 minutes

CAN THIS   BUMPER CROP

After I started pickling snap beans with Asian-inspired flavors, my love for Classic Dilly Beans (page 62) took a back seat. I use these pickles in everything from Bloody Marys to three-bean salads. With a bit of my homegrown horseradish and a sharp, tingly bite from the Szechuan peppercorns, these pickles are irresistible.

3½ pounds green and/or yellow snap beans (14 cups)

5 cups apple cider vinegar (5% acidity)

5 cups water

¼ cup soy sauce

3½ teaspoons Szechuan peppercorns, divided

7 garlic cloves

7 dried Japones chiles or other hot chiles

7 slices peeled horseradish root

14 slices peeled fresh ginger

1. Snap off the bean ends, then snap each bean so that it is no more than 4 inches long, reserving any smaller pieces for eating fresh. Clean and sanitize seven wide-mouth pint jars (See "Canning, Step by Step," page 6). In a large saucepan, bring the vinegar, water, and soy sauce just to a boil.

2. Grab one hot jar at a time with a pot holder and hold it at a 45-degree angle. Put ½ teaspoon peppercorns, 1 garlic clove, 1 chile, 1 slice of horseradish, and 2 slices of ginger in each jar. Pack in the beans so that they will be vertical when you set the jars upright.

3. Ladle in the hot brine, submerging the beans; leave ½ inch of headspace. If any beans stick up into the head-space, snap off the top ends until they are submerged in the brine. Wipe the rim and cap each jar with a two-piece canning lid. Add each jar to a boiling-water bath.

4. Process the pints in the boiling-water bath for 5 minutes, plus your altitude adjustment (see page 191). Store the jars in a dry, dark, cool place for at least 2 weeks before eating. The pickles are best eaten within a year.

Ingredient Tip: Szechuan peppercorns are actually the husks of dried berries from a Chinese shrub. They are readily available in Asian markets and spice shops, but in a pinch you can substitute black peppercorns, which are more potent, more common, and originate in Southwest India.

Savory Refrigerator Beets

Makes 1 pint

Prep time: 10 minutes, plus 30 minutes cooling time

Cook time: 3 minutes
Curing time: 2 days

Beets are often pickled whole or in thick slices that need to sit at least a week before they are ready to eat. By dicing the beets, you can eat them more quickly than canned beets, and they will keep longer in the refrigerator than ultra-thin quick-pickled beets. Although I generally prefer wide-mouth jars for pickles, the shoulders of a narrow-mouth jar here prevent the beets from floating to the surface.

1 pound beets, roasted, peeled, and diced (1½ cups) (for roasting and peeling instructions, see Water Bath–Processed Beets, page 65)

1 garlic clove, minced

¾ teaspoon cumin seeds

¼ teaspoon yellow mustard seeds

¼ dried chile de árbol, crumbled

¾ cup red wine vinegar (5% acidity)

1½ tablespoons sugar

½ teaspoon Morton pickling salt

1 tablespoon extra-virgin olive oil, for serving (optional)

1. In a clean narrow-mouth pint jar, combine the roasted beets and garlic.

2. In a dry skillet over medium-low heat, toast the cumin seeds, mustard seeds, and crumbled chile, stirring constantly, for about 3 minutes, until the mustard seeds start to pop.

3. Pour the toasted spices into a small saucepan and add the vinegar, sugar, and salt. Bring the liquid to a boil, stirring to dissolve the sugar and salt.

4. Ladle the hot brine over the beets so that they are submerged but the brine is about ½ inch from the jar's rim. Cover loosely with a nonreactive lid and let sit until completely cooled, about 30 minutes. Tighten the lid and store in the refrigerator for at least 2 days before eating. The pickles will keep for at least 3 months. Just before serving, toss with olive oil, if desired.

Ingredient Tip: This recipe comes together quickly with roasted beets leftover from a dinner or another pickling session. You can take the roasted and toasted flavors one step further by smoking the beets and chile.

Water Bath–Processed Beets

Makes 7 pints

Prep time: 20 minutes
Cook time: 1 hour

Processing time: 30 minutes
Curing time: 3 weeks

CAN THIS   **BUMPER CROP**

With their long processing time, pickled beets sealed in a boiling-water bath hold their shape best when small and left whole. But if they're larger than 1½ inches in diameter, it's best to cut them into pieces or slices. Either way, they can be challenging to pack efficiently into jars, so don't be surprised by the amount of brine needed.

7 pounds (2-inch or smaller) beets, trimmed to leave ½ inch of the stem and root

6 cups apple cider vinegar (5% acidity)

3 cups water

¾ cup sugar

1½ teaspoons Morton pickling salt

1 teaspoon allspice berries

½ teaspoon black peppercorns

2 (4-inch) cinnamon sticks, broken into pieces

1. Preheat the oven to 425°F.

2. In a foil-covered baking dish, roast the beets for 45 minutes to 1 hour, until they're easily pierced with a fork but not mushy. Plunge them immediately into a large bowl of ice water, cut off the tops and bottoms, and rub or peel away the skin. Halve or quarter large beets, or cut all sizes into ¼-inch-thick slices.

3. Meanwhile, in a large saucepan, bring the vinegar, water, sugar, and salt to a boil, stirring to dissolve the sugar and salt. Tie the spices in a spice bag or piece of cheese-cloth and add them to the saucepan as the sugar starts to dissolve. Lower the heat and simmer, uncovered, for 10 minutes. Remove the spice bag.

4. Pack the beets into seven clean, hot wide-mouth pint jars. Ladle in the hot brine, submerging the beets; leave ½ inch of headspace. Remove any air bubbles with a bamboo or wooden chopstick and wipe each jar's rim. Cap the jars with two-piece canning lids.

5. Process the pints in a boiling-water bath for 30 minutes, plus your altitude adjustment (see page 191). Store the jars in a dry, dark, cool place for at least 3 weeks before eating. The pickles are best eaten within a year.

Ingredient Tip: I have sometimes found pickled beets to be overly sweet, so I created this recipe as a low-sugar version. The food safety of these pickles is assured by the vinegar-to-water ratio, with the sugar doing more for flavor than preservation.

Chinese-Inspired Carrots

Makes 1 pint

Prep time: 10 minutes, plus 30 minutes cooling time

Curing time: 3 days

This carrot pickle takes on the flavors typically found in Chinese five-spice blends the longer it sits in the refrigerator. But rather than coating the carrots in powder, which tends to separate and cloud the jar over time, it relies on whole spices to develop the flavor. If after 3 days you taste the pickle and find the spices to your liking, strain the brine and repack the jar with just the carrots and liquid.

3 medium carrots

1 garlic clove, smashed

¼ teaspoon Szechuan peppercorns

⅛ teaspoon whole cloves

1 (1-inch) cinnamon stick, crushed

1 star anise pod

½ cup unseasoned rice vinegar (4.3% acidity)

2 tablespoons bottled lemon juice (5% acidity)

6 tablespoons water

½ teaspoon Morton pickling salt

1. Cut the carrots into 4-inch or shorter lengths and then ½-inch-thick sticks.

2. Put the garlic, peppercorns, cloves, cinnamon stick, and star anise at the bottom of a clean wide-mouth pint jar. Tip the jar to a 45-degree angle. Pack in the carrot sticks so that they will be vertical when you set the jar upright.

3. In a small saucepan, bring the vinegar, lemon juice, water, and salt to a boil, stirring to dissolve the salt. Ladle the hot brine over the carrots so that they are submerged but the brine is about ½ inch from the jar's rim. Cover loosely with a nonreactive lid and let sit until completely cooled, about 30 minutes. Tighten the lid and store in the refrigerator for 3 days before eating. The pickles will keep in the refrigerator for about 3 months.

Switch Things Up: Other Asian-inspired flavorings work in this recipe. Replace the spices with a couple of slices of horseradish and ginger and a piece of dried chile for a hot pickle. For less licorice flavor, use less star anise or substitute a pinch of fennel seeds.

Taqueria Carrots

Makes 1 quart

Prep time: 20 minutes, plus 30 minutes cooling time

Cook time: 5 minutes
Curing time: 3 days

The long cooking time plus boiling-water-bath processing typical of canned pickled carrots steals their crispness. This recipe blanches the carrots just enough to let the vinegar penetrate, and then the pickles are stored in the refrigerator. Fresh carrots keep so well in a crisper drawer or, for a large harvest, a box of sand in an unheated mudroom, that I don't mind pickling a jar at a time.

13 cups water, divided

6 medium carrots, cut ½ inch thick at an angle (3 cups)

2 teaspoons Mexican-Inspired Spice Blend (page 17)

4 garlic cloves, smashed

½ small onion, thinly sliced (¼ cup)

2 large jalapeño peppers, cut into ¼-inch rings (scant ½ cup)

1 cup white wine vinegar (5% acidity)

1 teaspoon Morton pickling salt

1. In large saucepan, bring 12 cups of water to a boil. Add the carrots and blanch them for 2 minutes. Drain the carrots and plunge them into a large bowl of ice water; let sit, stirring occasionally, until completely cooled, about 30 minutes. Drain the carrots completely in a colander.

2. In the bottom of a clean wide-mouth quart jar, place the spice blend and garlic. Layer in the carrots, onion, and jalapeño rings.

3. In a small saucepan, bring the remaining 1 cup of water, the vinegar, and salt to a boil. Ladle the hot brine over the vegetables so that they are submerged but the brine is about ½ inch from the jar's rim. Cover loosely with a nonreactive lid and let sit until completely cooled. Tighten the lid and store in the refrigerator for 3 days before eating. The pickles will keep for about 1 month in the refrigerator.

Pickled Chive Blossoms

Makes 1 pint   **Prep time:** 5 minutes   **Curing time:** 5 days

This recipe creates two products at one time: unique, onion-flavored pickled chive blossoms and infused vinegar. Harvest the flowers while they're dry, and any insects can be removed by gentle shaking. Dew-kissed blossoms can be dunked several times in a bowl of water and then spread on a clean dish towel to dry before they are pickled. The chive blossoms will be pickled after 24 hours, but the vinegar's flavor will be too subtle. Five days is just right for both.

20 fresh chive blossoms or
  8 fresh garlic chive blossoms
1¾ cups white wine vinegar
  (5% acidity)

1. In a clean wide-mouth pint jar, pack as many blossoms as you can fit without crushing them. Pour the vinegar over the blossoms so that they are submerged but the brine is about 1 inch from the jar's rim. Screw on a non-reactive lid and let sit at room temperature for at least 24 hours and up to 5 days.

2. Strain out the pickled flowers and set them aside to eat. Pour the vinegar into a clean 16-ounce glass bottle and cap it with a nonreactive lid. It will keep in the refrigerator for up to 6 months.

Ingredient Tip: Eat the pickled flowers raw in salads, tossed with glazed vegetables, or minced and folded into mashed potatoes. The vinegar is a delicious base for light salad dressings, marinades, and quick pickles (use with Tangy Radish Rounds, page 48).

Pickled Garlic Cloves

Makes 1 half-pint   **Prep time:** 15 minutes   **Curing time:** 2 weeks
                          Cook time: 5 minutes

CAN THIS

The acidity of vinegar does wonderful things to garlic, converting the compound allicin (which gives garlic its harsh bite) to mellower compounds the longer it sits. Blanching makes it easier for the vinegar to penetrate the hard cloves and mellow its pungency more quickly. The quick dips in boiling then icy water also lets you easily remove the papery skins without crushing or otherwise damaging the cloves.

8 garlic heads (1 cup whole garlic cloves)

½ cup white wine vinegar (5% acidity)

2 teaspoons sugar

½ teaspoon Morton pickling salt

1. Break the heads of garlic into cloves, leaving any skins that don't naturally come free. Bring a large saucepan filled with water to a rolling boil. Put the unpeeled cloves in the water, return the water to a boil, and blanch for 30 to 60 seconds. Drain the cloves in a colander, then plunge them into a bowl of ice water. Let them sit until they are cool enough to handle.

2. Drain the cooled garlic cloves, then slip off their skins. Pack all the peeled cloves into a clean ½-pint jar.

3. In a small saucepan, bring the vinegar, sugar, and salt to a boil, stirring to dissolve the sugar and salt. Ladle the hot brine over the cloves so that they are submerged but the brine is about ½ inch from the jar's rim. Cover loosely with a nonreactive lid and let sit at room temperature for 24 hours. Tighten the lid and store in the refrigerator for at least 2 weeks before using. The pickles will keep for months in the refrigerator.

Switch Things Up: To can this recipe in a boiling-water bath, multiply it by the number of ½-pint jars you want. After filling the jars in step 3, wipe each jar's rim, cap the jars with two-piece canning lids, and process for 10 minutes, plus your altitude adjustment (see page 191).

Try It With: Pickled garlic adds crunch and zing to any appetizer tray. Chop and sauté the cloves with fresh vegetables or use them instead of garlic-stuffed olives in savory cocktails. Older garlic can turn blue-green in vinegar, but it's safe to eat. If the color bothers you, blend these cloves instead of fresh garlic into salad dressings or marinades.

Spring Giardiniera

Makes 1 quart

Prep time: 30 minutes, plus 30 minutes cooling time

Curing time: 3 days

Although most gardeners turn to mixed vegetable pickles to handle an overflow of summer produce, spring vegetables can receive the same treatment. Once the excitement over the first flush of fresh food wanes, asparagus, early broccoli, radishes, and scallions can turn into bright, crisp pickles. By that time, it's likely that carrots need thinning, garlic scapes are beginning to curl, and herbs are ready for their first trim.

15 medium asparagus spears (12 ounces), sliced into 1-inch lengths (2 cups)

1 small bunch broccolini or broccoli rabe (4 ounces), trimmed of leaves and cut into 2-inch lengths (2 cups)

6 salad radishes, quartered (½ cup)

1 small carrot, cut into 2-inch lengths (¼ cup)

4 scallions, white parts only, cut into 2-inch lengths (¼ cup)

4 (6-inch) garlic scapes, thinly sliced or 2 garlic cloves, thinly sliced

1 teaspoon fresh thyme or ½ teaspoon dried thyme

½ teaspoon mustard seeds

1 bay leaf

1 cup white wine vinegar (5% acidity)

½ cup water

1 teaspoon Morton pickling salt

1. In a large bowl, combine the asparagus, broccolini, radishes, carrot, scallions, and garlic scapes. Toss to mix.

2. In the bottom of a clean wide-mouth quart jar, place the thyme, mustard seeds, and bay leaf. Fill the jar one-third full with vegetables, then tap it gently on the counter to settle the vegetables into place. Repeat the packing and settling two-thirds from the top and at the shoulders of the jar.

3. In a small saucepan, bring the vinegar, water, and salt to a boil, stirring to dissolve the salt. Ladle the brine over the vegetables so that they are submerged but the brine is about ½ inch from the jar's rim. Cover loosely with a nonreactive lid and let sit until completely cooled, about 30 minutes. Tighten the nonreactive lid and store in the refrigerator for 3 days before eating. The pickles will keep for weeks in the refrigerator.

Switch Things Up: To can this recipe in a boiling-water bath, multiply it by the number of quart jars you want and swap the ½ cup water for more vinegar. After filling the jars in step 3, wipe each jar's rim, cap the jars with two-piece canning lids, and process for 10 minutes, plus your altitude adjustment (see page 191). The seasonings can also be adjusted to taste or even enhanced with a mix like Sweet-Savory Spice Blend (page 16).

Summer Giardiniera

Makes 1 quart   **Prep time:** 30 minutes, plus 30 minutes cooling time   **Curing time:** 3 days

CAN THIS

Giardiniera has its roots in summer gardens in Italy but spread with immigrants to Chicago, where it exploded into a fiery condiment featuring crunchy pickled vegetables soaked in oil. For home canning, I prefer to skip the oil and stick with the crisp, vinegar-laced mixed vegetables I enjoyed in northern Italy. More antipasto than condiment, this version can be adapted to use what you have in your garden.

1 medium zucchini cubed (1 cup)

1 small onion, quartered (1 cup)

1 medium carrot, cut into ¼-inch rounds (½ cup)

⅛ small head cauliflower, cut into florets (½ cup)

¼ large bell pepper, cut into ¾-inch squares (½ cup)

1 Anaheim chile, cut into ¼-inch rings (⅓ cup)

1 Fresno chile or hotter chile, cut into ⅛-inch rings (3 tablespoons)

1 tablespoon minced fresh oregano

1½ teaspoons minced fresh tarragon

½ teaspoon fresh thyme

2 garlic cloves

1 bay leaf

1 cup white wine vinegar (5% acidity)

½ cup water

1 teaspoon Morton pickling salt

1. In a large bowl, combine the zucchini, onion, carrot, cauliflower, bell pepper, and both chiles; toss to mix. Sprinkle with the oregano, tarragon, and thyme then mix again.

2. In the bottom of a clean wide-mouth quart jar, place the garlic and bay leaf. Fill the jar one-third with vegetables; then tap it gently on the counter to settle the vegetables into place. Repeat the packing and settling two-thirds from the top and at the shoulders of the jar.

3. In a small saucepan, bring the vinegar, water, and salt to a boil, stirring to dissolve the salt. Ladle the brine over the vegetables so that they are submerged but the brine is about ½ inch from the jar's rim. Cover loosely with a nonreactive lid and let sit until completely cooled, about 30 minutes. Tighten the lid and store in the refrigerator for 3 days before eating. The pickles will keep for weeks in the refrigerator.

Switch Things Up: This recipe can be canned in the same manner as Spring Giardiniera (see Tip, page 70), first replacing the ½ cup water with vinegar. If you don't have one of the fresh herbs, substitute dried leaves at a half or a third of the given amount.

Gari (Sushi Ginger)

Makes 1 half-pint   **Prep time:** 10 minutes   **Cook time:** 5 minutes
Curing time: 1 to 4 weeks

Even if you don't make sushi at home, a jar of gari should be a staple of your refrigerator's condiment shelf for takeout, sushi bowls, and salad topping and dressings. Although you may be inclined to drop the sugar, don't leave it out: Both ginger and vinegar pack a powerful punch that's balanced by a little sweetness. As with garlic, blanching mellows the ginger slices, as does waiting at least a week before digging in.

4 (4-inch) pieces preferably young, fresh ginger (4 ounces)

½ cup unseasoned rice vinegar (4.3% acidity)

2½ tablespoons sugar

Pinch Morton pickling salt

1. Use the edge of a small spoon to peel the ginger, then cut off the rough, unpeeled ends with a sharp knife. Using a mandoline or a very sharp knife, cut the ginger into nearly translucent slices. Cut young ginger parallel to the fibers. If the ginger is mature and tougher, cut it crosswise into coins.

2. Fill a medium saucepan with water and bring it to a rolling boil. Add the ginger, return the water to a boil, and blanch for 30 to 60 seconds. Drain in a colander.

3. Put the vinegar, sugar, and salt in the empty saucepan and bring it just to a boil, stirring to dissolve the sugar and salt.

4. When the ginger is cool enough to handle, pack it into a clean, hot ½-pint jar. Ladle the hot brine over the slices so that they are submerged but the brine is about ½ inch from the jar's rim. Remove any air bubbles with a bamboo or wooden chopstick. Cover loosely with a nonreactive lid and let sit at room temperature for 3 to 4 hours. Tighten the lid and store in the refrigerator for at least 1 week before eating. The pickle will keep for at least 6 months in the refrigerator.

Ingredient Tip: Thin-skinned young ginger can be peeled with a fingernail and has the best texture and flavor when pickled but can be hard to find; look for it in the spring in an Asian market. Young ginger can be sliced with the grain, but cutting mature ginger that way leaves tough, stringy fibers. Cutting older ginger against the grain hides that undesirable texture.

Misozuke (Miso Pickle)

Makes 3 cups   **Prep time:** 10 minutes, plus 1 hour salting time   **Curing time:** 3 days

This pickling bed, made with a lower-salt white miso base than Miso Asazuke (page 47), works more slowly but can be reused for up to a month. The miso will last longer if you pull as much moisture as possible from the fresh vegetables. Other vegetables can be miso-pickled, as can fruit, fish, and tofu. Be sure to reserve this bed for produce and create a separate bed if you want to pickle proteins.

1 large carrot, peeled and cut into ¼-inch rounds (¾ cup)

1 (2-inch) piece daikon radish, peeled and cut into half-moons (¾ cup)

1 small turnip, peeled and cut into quarter- or half-moons (¾ cup)

1½ teaspoons Diamond Crystal kosher salt

1 cup white miso

2 tablespoons sake

1 teaspoon sugar

1. Put the vegetables in a colander set over a bowl, toss with the salt, and let their excess moisture drain for 1 hour. Rinse, drain again, and pat dry with a dish towel.

2. In a small measuring cup, mix together the miso, sake, and sugar. In a clean, shallow, flat-bottomed container with a lid, spread a thin layer of the miso mixture. Top this with a layer of vegetables, then repeat, alternating the miso and vegetable layers until all the vegetables are coated in miso. Spread the remaining miso over the top, ensuring the uppermost layer of vegetables is completely covered. Store the lidded container in the refrigerator for at least 3 days and up to 1 month.

3. To serve, remove the vegetables from the pickling bed, wiping excess miso back into the pickling bed with your fingers. If they seem too salty, rinse off the remaining miso under cool running water and pat the vegetables dry. Cut into smaller pieces or thin strips if desired.

Switch Things Up: If you don't plan on heavily reusing your pickling bed, you can layer cheesecloth between the vegetables and miso that can then be peeled away. This saves you from having to rinse the vegetables, but you'll lose some of the miso each time you clean the cloth.

Cocktail Onions

Makes 1 pint

Prep time: 20 minutes, plus 8 hours salting time

Cook time: 5 minutes
Curing time: 2 days

Although I adore homemade cocktail mixers and garnishes, it took me a long time to pickle cocktail onions. I grow pearl onions only by accident in my garden, the result of a poor harvest. I tuck pickled beans, asparagus, and garlic into my Bloody Marys and prefer olives to onions in gin cocktails. But it's worth buying a bag of pearl onions for these cuties, particularly if you love an evening Gibson.

2 cups fresh pearl onions (10 ounces)

4 cups boiling water

1 cup cool water, divided

3 tablespoons Diamond Crystal kosher salt, divided

½ cup white wine vinegar (5% acidity)

¼ cup unseasoned rice vinegar (4.3% acidity)

2 tablespoons sugar

6 coriander seeds, crushed

6 black peppercorns, crushed

3 juniper berries, crushed

1. Put the onions in a medium heatproof bowl and pour in the boiling water. Let sit for 1 minute, then drain the onions and plunge them immediately into a bowl of cold water. Cut off the root and top tips with a sharp knife, then slip off the outer skins.

2. In a small measuring cup, whisk together ¾ cup of cool water and 2 tablespoons of salt, stirring until the salt dissolves. In a clean wide-mouth pint jar, pack the onions tightly. Pour the salt brine over the onions, cover loosely with a nonreactive lid, and let sit at room temperature overnight.

3. In a small saucepan, bring the remaining ¼ cup of cool water, the remaining tablespoon of salt, and the white wine vinegar, rice vinegar, and sugar to a boil, stirring until the salt and sugar are dissolved. Add the onions, lower the heat, and simmer for 2 minutes. Remove the pan from the heat and let sit for about 30 minutes, until cooled to room temperature. Meanwhile, transfer the onions into a colander to drain; rinse them under running cool water, then drain again.

4. In the bottom of the pint jar, place the coriander, peppercorns, and juniper berries. Pack in the onions, then ladle the brine over them so that they are submerged but the brine is about ½ inch from the jar's rim. Screw on a nonreactive lid and store in the refrigerator for at least 2 days before using. The pickles will keep for months in the refrigerator.

Ingredient Tip: The blend of white wine and rice vinegars balance the vermouth in a Gibson while adding a touch of sweetness. I chose these spices for the jar because they bring out the botanicals in my favorite gins.

Switch Things Up: Grab frozen, pre-peeled pearl onions for a quick-pickle cocktail garnish; you'll need about 7 ounces for a full recipe. They won't have the long-lasting crispness of fresh onions, but they'll be ready to eat in about 8 hours. Skip the first two steps; instead, start by defrosting the frozen onions in a colander over a bowl in the refrigerator before continuing with step 3.

Pickled Nasturtium Seeds

Makes 1 half-pint

Prep time: 10 minutes, plus 20 minutes cooling and 3 days salting time

Curing time: 4 days

Brightly colored nasturtiums aren't just beautiful; they're also entirely edible. Their seeds, when pickled, become a northern gardener's replacement for capers. If you grow heaps of nasturtiums, you'll have no problem harvesting enough seeds in one session. If you come up short, you can brine them in stages, adding 3-day-soaked batches to the vinegar jar until it is full. Choose only soft, green pods for pickling; harder ones should be saved for planting next season.

½ cup nasturtium seeds

½ cup water

2¼ teaspoons Morton pickling salt

¾ cup white wine vinegar (5% acidity)

2 teaspoons sugar

1. In a clean ½-pint jar, pack the nasturtium seeds.

2. In a small saucepan, bring the water and salt to a boil, stirring to dissolve the salt. Ladle the brine over the seeds and let sit for about 20 minutes, until cooled to room temperature. Cover the jar with a lid and let the seeds soak at room temperature for 3 days, stirring occasionally to ensure they stay submerged.

3. Drain the soaked nasturtium seeds in a colander, rinse the jar, and put the seeds back in the jar.

4. In a small saucepan, bring the vinegar and sugar to a boil, stirring to dissolve the sugar. Ladle the hot brine over the nasturtium seeds so that they are submerged but the brine is about ½ inch from the jar's rim. Cover loosely with a nonreactive lid and let sit at room temperature for 24 hours. Tighten the lid and store in the refrigerator for at least 3 days before using. The nasturtium "capers" will keep for months in the refrigerator.

Ingredient Tip: Nasturtiums produce a chickpea-size seed after each blossom peaks. For eating, harvest them green as soon as the flower petals have fallen off; the more you pluck, the more flowers and seeds the plant will produce. The seeds smell of sulfur when first brined. The multiday soak reduces the stink, brings flower debris to the surface, and mellows the seeds' sharp bite. If you find the debris or smell is excessive, drain the seeds and re-cover them with fresh saltwater brine daily.

Fridge-Pickled Pepperoncini

Makes 1 pint

Prep time: 10 minutes, plus 30 minutes cooling time

Curing time: 2 to 4 weeks

Those little pickled peppers so popular alongside a sandwich from your favorite Italian deli can be easily made at home. The biggest challenge may be finding the right peppers. Pepperoncini are a specific chile variety, milder than many other peppers and smaller than most other mild peppers. The plants and peppers may also be sold as friggitello or Tuscan peppers. I pack them in narrow-mouth jars to help keep them submerged in their brine.

20 pepperoncini peppers (8 ounces)

¼ teaspoon coriander seeds

¼ teaspoon black peppercorns

1 garlic clove

1 bay leaf

½ cup apple cider vinegar (5% acidity)

½ cup water

1½ teaspoons Morton pickling salt

1 teaspoon sugar (optional)

1. Using a sharp knife, poke 1 or 2 holes in each pepper.

2. In the bottom of a clean narrow-mouth pint jar, place the coriander, peppercorns, garlic, and bay leaf. Tip the jar at a 45-degree angle, then pack in the peppers so they will be vertical when you set the jar upright.

3. In a small saucepan, bring the vinegar, water, salt, and sugar (if using) to a boil, stirring to dissolve the salt and sugar. Ladle the hot brine over the peppers so that they are submerged but the brine is about ½ inch from the jar's rim. Cover loosely with a nonreactive lid and let sit until completely cooled, about 30 minutes. Tighten the lid and store in the refrigerator for 2 to 4 weeks before eating. The pickles will keep for months in the refrigerator.

Don't Forget: Although these peppers are pickled whole, it's worth wearing rubber gloves while you handle and pack them, especially if you are highly sensitive to the capsaicin.

Apple-Sweetened Yellow Onions

Makes 1 quart

Prep time: 10 minutes, plus 20 minutes salting and 30 minutes cooling time

Cook time: 1 minute
Curing time: 24 hours

A little sugar and apple cider vinegar give these pickled onions a slightly sweet flavor without turning them into a candied savory spread. They remind me of the sautéed apples and onions my mom liked to serve when I was growing up. They're delicious on grilled portobello mushrooms, in potato salad, and under poached eggs.

3 medium (1 pound) yellow onions, cut into ¼-inch rings (3⅓ cups)

1 teaspoon Morton pickling salt

1½ cups apple cider vinegar (5% acidity)

½ cup water

1½ teaspoons sugar

½ teaspoon red pepper flakes

1 teaspoon cardamom seeds (not pods)

1. In a colander, toss the onion rings with the salt and let sit for 20 minutes.

2. In a small saucepan, bring the vinegar, water, and sugar to a boil, stirring until the sugar dissolves.

3. Gently squeeze excess liquid from the onions with your hands. Stir the onions into the brine, lower the heat to medium, and simmer for 1 minute.

4. In the bottom of a clean wide-mouth quart jar, place the red pepper flakes and cardamom seeds. Pack the onions into the jar, using tongs to lift them from the hot brine. Ladle the brine over the onions so that they are submerged but the brine is about ½ inch from the jar's rim. Remove any air bubbles with a bamboo or wooden chopstick. Cover loosely with a nonreactive lid and let sit until completely cooled, about 30 minutes. Tighten the lid and store in the refrigerator for at least 24 hours before eating. The pickles will keep for up to 1 month in the refrigerator.

Curried Green Tomatoes

Makes 1 pint

Prep time: 10 minutes, plus 6 hours salting and 30 minutes cooling time

Curing time: 3 weeks

These pickles break my general rule about using whole, not ground, spices in pickles. Homemade curry powder in particular lends a lovely flavor without turning to sludge at the bottom of the jar the longer it sits. If you are making your own masala, you can always leave enough as a whole spice blend to use in this recipe; I still recommend toasting it before adding it to the jar.

3 medium (1 pound) green tomatoes, cored and cut into ¼-inch slices (1½ cups)

1 small onion, cut into paper-thin rings (1 cup)

1 tablespoon Morton pickling salt

Ice cubes

½ cup apple cider vinegar (5% acidity)

3 tablespoons water

1½ teaspoons brown sugar

1 teaspoon curry powder

2 slices peeled fresh ginger

1. In a medium bowl, layer the tomatoes and onion with the salt. Cover with ice cubes and a dish towel and refrigerate for 6 hours or overnight.

2. Drain the vegetables in a colander; rinse them under cool running water, then drain again.

3. In a small saucepan, bring the vinegar, water, sugar, and curry powder to a boil, stirring to dissolve the sugar.

4. In a clean wide-mouth pint jar, layer the tomato and onion, along with the ginger. Ladle the hot brine over the vegetables so that they are submerged but the brine is about ½ inch from the jar's rim. Cover loosely with a nonreactive lid and let sit until completely cooled, about 30 minutes. Tighten the lid and store in the refrigerator for at least 3 weeks before eating. The pickles will keep for months in the refrigerator.

Ingredient Tip: Firmer green tomatoes make firmer pickles; be sure to avoid frostbitten ones at the end of the season. It's worth culling tomatoes with a 3-inch or larger diameter, because whole tomato slices will look prettier and hold up better in the jar.

Double-Spiced Zucchini

Makes 1 pint

Prep time: 15 minutes, plus 2 hours salting and cooling time

Curing time: 1 week

When temperatures spike, summer squash plants, both zucchini and yellow crookneck, can pump out pounds of produce. After years of trying a boiling-water bath and then pasteurizing at a lower temperature, I realized that only refrigerator pickles would keep zucchini crisp. Small, young zucchini make the best pickles and are crispest in the first a couple of weeks. The double spicing comes from ground cumin and fresh chile boosting the cumin seeds and dried chile in the pickling spice.

3 small (6-inch) zucchini, cut into ¼-inch rounds (1½ cups)

½ small onion, sliced into paper-thin rings (¼ cup)

2¼ teaspoons Morton pickling salt, divided

Ice cubes

⅓ cup water

⅓ cup apple cider vinegar (5% acidity)

½ teaspoon honey

Pinch ground cumin

1 teaspoon Mexican-Inspired Spice Blend (page 17)

1 garlic clove, smashed

1 serrano chile

1. In a small bowl, toss the vegetables with 2 teaspoons of salt. Cover with ice cubes and a dish towel and let sit at room temperature for 2 hours.

2. Meanwhile, in a small saucepan, bring the remaining ¼ teaspoon of salt and the water, vinegar, honey, and ground cumin to a boil, stirring until the salt and honey dissolve. Remove the pan from the heat and let sit for about 30 minutes, until the brine has cooled to room temperature.

3. Drain the squash and onions in a colander; rinse them under cool running water, then drain again before patting them dry with a dish towel.

4. Dry the bowl, return the vegetables to it, and toss them with the spice blend.

5. In a clean wide-mouth pint jar, layer the spiced zucchini and onion, tucking the garlic and chile down the side as you go. Ladle the brine over the vegetables so that they are submerged but the brine is about ½ inch from the jar's rim. Screw on a nonreactive lid and store in the refrigerator for at least 1 week before eating. The pickles will keep for weeks in the refrigerator.

Bread and Butter–Style Summer Squash

Makes 1 quart

Prep time: 15 minutes, plus 2 hours salting and cooling time

Curing time: 2 weeks

If you're a fan of bread-and-butter cucumber pickles, you'll want to add those spices to your zucchini, too. The cold temperature and vinegar preserve the zucchini's crispness, but these pickles won't keep as long as shelf-stable ones run through a boiling-water bath. With the raw squash covered by room-temperature brine, they'll taste best if they sit longer before the first bite than most refrigerator pickles.

6 small (6-inch) zucchini (3 cups)

½ small onion (¼ cup)

2½ teaspoons Morton pickling salt, divided

Ice cubes

1 cup apple cider vinegar (5% acidity)

¼ cup water

2 tablespoons honey

2 teaspoons Bread-and-Butter Spice Blend (page 17)

2 garlic cloves

2 slices peeled horseradish root

1. Using a mandoline or very sharp knife, cut the zucchini into ¼-inch-thick slices and the onion into paper-thin rings. In a small bowl, toss the vegetables with 2 teaspoons of salt. Cover with ice cubes and a dish towel and let sit at room temperature for 2 hours.

2. Meanwhile, in a small saucepan, bring the vinegar, water, honey, spice blend, and the remaining ½ teaspoon of salt to a boil, stirring to dissolve the honey and salt. Lower the heat, cover, and simmer for 5 minutes. Remove the pan from the heat and let sit for about 30 minutes, until the brine has cooled to room temperature.

3. Drain the squash and onion in a colander; rinse them under cool running water, then drain again.

4. In the bottom of a clean wide-mouth quart jar, place the garlic and horseradish slices, then layer in the zucchini and onion. Ladle the brine over the vegetables so that they are submerged but the brine is about ½ inch from the jar's rim. Screw on a nonreactive lid and store in the refrigerator for 2 weeks before eating. The pickles will keep for up to 3 months in the refrigerator.

Ingredient Tip: If you don't grow your own squash and keep a close eye on your plants, you may struggle to find small zucchini. If each squash is 8 ounces, you might only fit two in a jar. The giants are best grated and frozen for zucchini bread and savory pancakes.

Herbes de Provence Zucchini

Makes 1 pint

Prep time: 15 minutes, plus 2 hours salting and 30 minutes cooling time

Curing time: 2 weeks

When I'm grilling or sautéing zucchini, I often sprinkle on a blend of fresh or dried herbs, so it seemed natural to put these into a zucchini pickle. Although commercial variations of this French classic abound, you can free-form the seasonings with a teaspoon of home-dried herbs or a tablespoon of whatever is fresh in your garden, or you can make your own French-inspired blend.

1 large zucchini, quartered and cut into 4-inch spears (1⅔ cups)

2 medium shallots, quartered (¼ cup)

2 teaspoons Morton pickling salt, divided

Ice cubes

⅓ cup white wine vinegar (5% acidity)

⅓ cup water

2 teaspoons sugar

1 teaspoon herbes de Provence

1. In a small bowl, toss the zucchini and shallots with 1½ teaspoons of salt. Cover with ice cubes and a dish towel and let sit at room temperature for 2 hours.

2. Drain the zucchini and shallots in a colander; rinse them under cool running water, then drain again.

3. In a small saucepan, bring the vinegar, water, sugar, and the remaining ½ teaspoon of salt to a boil, stirring until the sugar and salt dissolve.

4. Dry the bowl, return the zucchini and shallots to it, then toss them with the herbes de Provence.

5. Tip a clean wide-mouth pint jar at a 45-degree angle, then pack in the zucchini and shallots so that the spears will be vertical when you set the jar upright. Ladle the hot brine over the vegetables so that they are submerged but the brine is about ½ inch from the jar's rim. Cover loosely with a nonreactive lid and let sit until completely cooled, about 30 minutes. Tighten the lid and store in the refrigerator for at least 2 weeks before eating. The pickles will keep for weeks in the refrigerator.

Ingredient Tip: If you'll be making these pickles often, you can mix up your own herbes de Provence blend. My favorite mixture uses equal parts thyme, savory, marjoram, basil, and fennel, with just a little sage, rosemary, and lavender added in for some true South-of-France flavor.

Fermented Red Onions, page 114

Half-Sour Dill Pickles, page 104

Fermented Pickles

Sauerkraut

Makes 1 half-gallon   **Prep time:** 30 minutes   **Curing time:** 1 to 6 weeks

BUMPER CROP

For most people, the word *sauerkraut* conjures images of plump, sizzling bratwurst alongside pickled cabbage, a pairing said to bring luck when eaten New Year's Day. In fact, the traditional ingredients in sauerkraut can vary by region or be as basic as cabbage and salt. Mix them up, then watch the natural bacteria go to work, eating sugars and creating lactic acid to preserve and flavor the cabbage. The technique has varied over the centuries, from sliced cabbage salted and stuffed in barrels to this contemporary method using a glass jar.

1 large (3-pound) head green
  or red cabbage
4 tablespoons Diamond
  Crystal kosher salt, divided

1. Set aside the cabbage's loose outer leaves. Place the stem end on a cutting board. Use a sharp knife to cut the cabbage down to the stem in quarters, then cut out the pieces of solid core. Lay each wedge flat-side down on the cutting board and cut it into thin strips.

2. In a large, wide bowl, place about half of the shredded cabbage. Sprinkle it with 2 tablespoons of salt, then toss with your hands or a pair of large spoons. Add the remaining cabbage and 2 tablespoons of salt and toss again, pressing and squeezing to release liquid.

3. In a clean ½-gallon jar or crock, firmly pack the cabbage and liquid. Cover the surface with a whole cabbage leaf, top with a weight, and cover the fermenting vessel, preferably with an air lock. Let sit in a dark, cool place to cure.

4. After 24 hours, check that the surface layer is submerged. If it's exposed, add enough brine with a 2.5% concentration (see the Brine Concentration chart on page 12) to submerge the cabbage. Continue to check the fermentation daily, releasing air bubbles over the first 3 days. Top off with brine and skim off any filmy surface layer as needed.

5. Taste after 1 week of curing; continue fermenting an additional 2 to 5 weeks as needed, until the sauerkraut reaches your preferred flavor. Store the finished sauerkraut in a glass container with a nonreactive lid in the refrigerator. As long as it stays submerged in its brine, it will keep for months.

Don't Forget: If this is your first time fermenting vegetables, review "Fermentation, Step by Step" (page 9) for more detailed steps and "Outfit Your Kitchen" (page 19) for descriptions of some of the tools used here.

Kvashenaya Kapusta
(Russian-Inspired Soured Cabbage)

Makes 1 half-gallon   **Prep time:** 15 minutes   **Curing time:** 4 to 5 days at room temperature, plus 1 to 7 days refrigerated

BUMPER CROP

I first tried Russian versions of sauerkraut when I lived in St. Petersburg. They never tasted the same; almost every Russian family had its own sweet-and-sour cabbage variation. I love the cranberries bleeding color and fruitiness into the jar. Russians prefer a juicy white cabbage for fermenting, but in the United States you're more likely to find denser green heads.

1 medium (2¾-pound) head green or white cabbage

4 tablespoons Diamond Crystal kosher salt, divided

2 medium carrots, grated (1 cup)

1½ teaspoons sugar

2 teaspoons caraway seeds (optional)

½ cup (2 ounces) fresh or frozen cranberries (optional)

1. Set aside the cabbage's loose outer leaves. Place the stem end on a cutting board. Use a sharp knife to cut the cabbage down to the stem in quarters, then cut out the pieces of solid core. Lay each wedge flat-side down on the cutting board and cut it into thin strips.

2. In a large, wide bowl, put about half of the shredded cabbage and sprinkle and toss it with 2 tablespoons of salt. Add the remaining cabbage and 2 tablespoons of salt and toss again. Add the grated carrots, sugar, and caraway seeds (if using) and toss a final time, pressing and squeezing to release liquid. Fold in the cranberries (if using).

3. In a clean ½-gallon jar or crock, firmly pack the vegetables and liquid. Cover the surface with a whole cabbage leaf, top with a weight, and cover the fermenting vessel, preferably with an air lock. Let sit in a dark, cool place to cure.

4. After 24 hours, check that the surface layer is submerged. If it's exposed, add enough brine with a 2.5% concentration (see the Brine Concentration chart on page 12) to submerge the vegetables. Continue to check the fermentation daily, releasing air bubbles over the first 3 days. Top off with brine and skim off any filmy surface layer as needed.

5. Taste after 4 to 5 days of curing to check that the soured cabbage has reached your preferred flavor. Store the soured cabbage in a glass container with a nonreactive lid in the refrigerator at least 1 day before eating. As long as it stays submerged in its brine, it will keep for 2 to 3 months in the refrigerator.

Ingredient Tip: If you're struggling to generate juices from a cabbage, more pressure can be added by tamping it with a potato masher or kraut pounder. Although you can use fresh or frozen cranberries, avoid dried ones; they won't release juice into the jar.

Apple and Cabbage Kraut

Makes 1 half-gallon   **Prep time:** 15 minutes   **Curing time:** 1 to 6 weeks

BUMPER CROP

This recipe puts a sweeter spin on classic sauerkraut. I make this with a storage cabbage variety, which ripens in the garden as apples turn sweet in the orchard. Freshly picked cabbage can gush liquid, but store-bought or stored heads may need brine. I shred the cabbage with a knife and grate the apple, skin on, with a large-hole cheese grater.

1 medium (2¾-pound) head green cabbage

4 tablespoons Diamond Crystal kosher salt, divided

1 medium apple, grated (1 cup)

2 teaspoons juniper berries, lightly crushed

1. Set aside the cabbage's loose outer leaves. Place the stem end on a cutting board. Use a sharp knife to cut the cabbage down to the stem in quarters, then cut out the pieces of solid core. Lay each wedge flat-side down on the cutting board and cut it into thin strips.

2. In a large, wide bowl, put about half of the shredded cabbage and sprinkle and toss it with 2 tablespoons of salt. Add the remaining cabbage and 2 tablespoons of salt and toss again. Add the grated apple and juniper berries and toss a final time, pressing and squeezing to release liquid.

3. In a clean ½-gallon jar or crock, firmly pack the cabbage and liquid. Cover the surface with a whole cabbage leaf, top with a weight, and cover the fermenting vessel, preferably with an air lock. Let sit in a dark, cool place to cure.

4. After 24 hours, check that the surface layer is submerged. If it's exposed, add enough brine with a 2.5% concentration (see the Brine Concentration chart on page 12) to submerge the cabbage. Continue to check the fermentation daily, releasing air bubbles over first 3 days. Top off with brine and skim off any filmy surface layer as needed.

5. Taste after 1 week of curing; continue fermenting an additional 2 to 5 weeks as needed, until the kraut reaches your preferred flavor. Store the finished kraut in a glass container with a nonreactive lid in the refrigerator. As long as it stays submerged in its brine, it will keep for months.

Switch Things Up: For a pretty variation, use red cabbage and a pinkish-fleshed apple in this recipe; they will turn the kraut bright pink. For another variation, the apple and juniper berries can be swapped in equal portions for yellow or red onion and caraway seeds.

Classic Kimchi

Makes 1 half-gallon   **Prep time:** 30 minutes, plus 6 hours salting time   **Curing time:** 3 to 12 days

I first started fermenting green cabbage with kimchi flavorings (see Green Cabbage Kimchi, page 98), because that's what was growing in my garden. It's delicious, but you'll get the signature texture by using napa cabbage. This recipe modernizes some traditional techniques and aims for moderate spiciness so that the kimchi can be eaten on its own or as part of an otherwise mild meal. Boost the heat or cut it back to suit your tastes.

1 large (2½-pound) head napa cabbage

6 cups unchlorinated water

5½ tablespoons Diamond Crystal kosher salt, divided

5 garlic cloves, minced or grated

1½ tablespoons peeled, grated fresh ginger

1 tablespoon sugar

3 tablespoons gochugaru (Korean red pepper flakes) or 2 tablespoons Anaheim red pepper flakes

2 teaspoons doenjang (fermented soybean paste) (optional)

1 (5-inch) piece daikon radish, cut into thin matchsticks (1¾ cups)

6 scallions, white part only, cut into ¾-inch pieces (⅓ cup)

1. Set aside at least 1 loose outer cabbage leaf. Lay the cabbage flat on a cutting board. Cut it lengthwise with a very sharp knife, then cut the solid core from each half. Cut the cabbage into 2-inch pieces and put them in a large, wide bowl.

2. In a large measuring cup, whisk together the water and 4½ tablespoons of salt, stirring until the salt dissolves. Pour the brine over the cabbage. Weigh it down with a plate, ensuring it is submerged, and let sit at room temperature for 6 hours to overnight.

3. Strain the brine through a colander set over the large measuring cup, then return the cabbage to the bowl, reserving the brine. In a medium bowl, mix the remaining 1 tablespoon of salt with the garlic, ginger, and sugar. Mix in the red pepper flakes and soybean paste (if using). Add the daikon and scallions and toss to coat. Using a rubber spatula, scrape the spiced vegetables into the cabbage, then fold together until thoroughly coated.

4. Using gloved hands, firmly pack the kimchi into a clean ½-gallon jar or crock. Cover the surface with a whole cabbage leaf, then add enough reserved brine to submerge the vegetables; store extra brine in a small lidded jar. Top the vegetables with a weight, and cover the fermenting vessel, preferably with an air lock. Let sit in a dark, cool place to cure.

5. After 24 hours, start to check the fermentation daily, releasing air bubbles over the first 2 days. Top off with brine and skim off any filmy surface layer as needed.

6. Taste after 3 to 6 days of curing; continue fermenting an additional 3 to 6 days as needed, until the kimchi reaches your preferred flavor. Store the finished kimchi in a glass container with a nonreactive lid in the refrigerator. As long as it stays submerged in its brine, it will keep for up to 6 months.

Ingredient Tip: For a true kimchi flavor, seek out Korean red pepper flakes at an Asian market. For flavoring, look for fermented soy paste to keep the kimchi vegan; fish sauce is another traditional tangy flavoring.

Bok Choy–Radish Kimchi

Makes 1 quart

Prep time: 30 minutes, plus 6 hours salting time

Curing time: 2 to 8 days

Make this kimchi when it's time to harvest early-season vegetables. Baby bok choy varieties mature about the same time as salad radishes, three to four weeks after planting, and early leaves can be cut, a few from each plant, from a bed of larger varieties.

2 pounds bok choy (8 cups stems)

12 salad radishes, thinly sliced (1 cup)

6 cups unchlorinated water

4½ tablespoons plus 2½ teaspoons Diamond Crystal kosher salt, divided

2 tablespoons gochugaru (Korean red pepper flakes) or ¼ teaspoon red pepper flakes

2 teaspoons sugar

1 teaspoon peeled, grated fresh ginger

2 garlic cloves, minced

8 scallions, white part only, cut into ¾-inch pieces (½ cup)

1. Trim off the hard ends of the bok choy stalks, then cut off most of the leaves, setting aside 1 large leaf and reserving the rest for another use. Cut the remaining stems into 1½-inch pieces.

2. In a large, wide bowl, put the bok choy stems and all the sliced radishes.

3. In a large measuring cup, whisk together the water and 4½ tablespoons of salt, stirring until the salt dissolves. Pour the brine over the vegetables. Weigh them down with a plate, ensuring they are submerged, and let sit at room temperature for 6 hours to overnight.

4. Strain the brine through a colander set over the large measuring cup, then return the vegetables to the large bowl, reserving both the brine and the vegetables. In a medium bowl, mix the remaining 2½ teaspoons of salt with the red pepper flakes, sugar, ginger, and garlic. Add the scallions and toss to coat. Using a rubber spatula, scrape the scallions into the salted vegetables, then fold together until thoroughly coated.

5. Using gloved hands, firmly pack the vegetables into a clean quart jar. Cover the surface with a whole bok choy leaf, then add enough reserved brine to submerge the vegetables; store extra brine in a small lidded jar. Top

the vegetables with a weight, and cover the fermenting vessel, preferably with an air lock. Let sit in a dark, cool place to cure.

6. After 24 hours, start to check the fermentation daily, releasing air bubbles over the first 2 days. Top off with brine and skim off any filmy surface layer as needed.

7. Taste after 2 days of curing; continue fermenting an additional 4 to 6 days as needed, until the kimchi reaches your preferred flavor. Store the finished kimchi in a glass container with a nonreactive lid in the refrigerator. As long as it stays submerged in its brine, it will keep for weeks.

Don't Forget: A kraut pounder, which might look like an oversized cocktail muddler, or a food plunger reduces contact while you're tamping down the jar contents.

Ingredient Tip: Korean pepper flakes have far less heat than common red pepper flakes, which are mostly cayenne. Anaheim pepper flakes, which may be available at a natural foods store, are more ideal for a 1:1 substitution.

Rhubarb Kimchi

Makes 1 quart   **Prep time:** 20 minutes   **Curing time:** 7 to 10 days

Being a cold-climate gardener, I grow lots of rhubarb; in my woodland yard, it flourishes all summer. I've loved the vegetable since childhood and am always on the lookout for new recipes. When I first heard of rhubarb kimchi, I knew it would become a regular in my fermentation rotation. This blend of rhubarb and spring onions spiked with sriracha makes an ideal first kimchi each year, before cabbage is in season.

1 pound rhubarb, thinly sliced (4 cups)

6 spring garlic stalks, thinly sliced (¾ cup) or 3 garlic cloves, minced

2 whole spring onions or 6 whole scallions, thinly sliced (¾ cup)

2 small carrots, grated (½ cup)

2 tablespoons Diamond Crystal kosher salt

2 tablespoons prepared or Scratch-Made Sriracha (page 130)

2 tablespoons peeled, grated fresh ginger

2 teaspoons sugar

2 teaspoons brown mustard seeds

1. In a large, wide bowl, put about half of the rhubarb, spring garlic, onions, and carrots. Sprinkle them with 1 tablespoon of salt, then toss with your hands or a pair of large spoons. Add the remaining vegetables and 1 tablespoon of salt and toss again, pressing and squeezing to release liquid.

2. In a medium bowl, mix the sriracha, ginger, sugar, and mustard seeds. Using a rubber spatula, scrape this paste into the large bowl with the salted vegetables, then fold together until thoroughly coated.

3. In a clean quart jar, firmly pack the kimchi and liquid. Cover the surface with a piece of cheesecloth, top with a weight, and cover the fermenting vessel, preferably with an air lock. Let sit in a dark, cool place to cure.

4. After 24 hours, check that the surface layer is submerged. If it's exposed, add enough brine with a 2.5% concentration (see the Brine Concentration chart on page 12) to submerge the vegetables. Continue to check the fermentation daily, releasing air bubbles over the first 3 days. Top off with brine and skim off any filmy surface layer as needed.

5. Taste after 5 days of curing; continue fermenting an additional 2 to 5 days as needed, until the kimchi reaches your preferred flavor. Store the finished kimchi in a glass container with a nonreactive lid in the refrigerator. As long as it stays submerged in its brine, it will keep for up to 6 months.

Don't Forget: Rhubarb leaves contain oxalic acid, which can cause kidney and other problems if eaten in large quantities. To avoid any risk, use cheesecloth or the leaf of another vegetable, like cabbage, to cover the kimchi.

Green Cabbage Kimchi

Makes 1 half-gallon   **Prep time:** 15 minutes   **Curing time:** 2 to 4 weeks

BUMPER CROP

How your garden grows can lead to interesting fusions of flavors. In the years my garden produces beautiful green cabbage but the napa cabbage bolts and becomes bitter, I don't have to miss out on classic kimchi. I simply mix the spicy flavors into shredded green cabbage. It builds a stronger sour flavor and the green cabbage shreds become softer the longer the ferment sits.

1 medium (2¾-pound) head green cabbage

6 whole scallions, cut into 2-inch pieces and slivered (¾ cup)

2 red jalapeño peppers or 1 Fresno chile, minced (3 tablespoons)

2 tablespoons peeled, minced fresh ginger

5 garlic cloves, minced

4 tablespoons Diamond Crystal kosher salt, divided

3 teaspoons sugar, divided

1. Set aside the cabbage's loose outer leaves. Place the stem end on a cutting board. Use a sharp knife to cut the cabbage down to the stem in quarters, then cut out the pieces of solid core. Lay each wedge flat-side down on the cutting board and cut it into thin strips.

2. In a large, wide bowl, put about half of the shredded cabbage and scallions. Add half of the peppers, ginger, and garlic, then toss to mix with gloved hands or a pair of large spoons. Sprinkle and toss it with 2 tablespoons of salt and 1½ teaspoons of sugar. Add the remaining vegetables, 2 tablespoons of salt, and 1½ teaspoons of sugar and toss again, pressing and squeezing to release liquid.

3. In a clean ½-gallon jar or crock, firmly pack the cabbage and liquid. Cover the surface with a whole cabbage leaf, top with a weight, and cover the fermenting vessel, preferably with an air lock. Let sit in a dark, cool place to cure.

4. After 24 hours, check that the surface layer is submerged. If it's exposed add enough brine with a 2.5% concentration (see the Brine Concentration chart on page 12) to submerge the cabbage. Continue to check the fermentation daily, releasing air bubbles over the first 3 days. Top off with brine and skim off any filmy surface layer as needed.

5. Taste after 2 weeks of curing; continue fermenting for an additional 2 weeks as needed, until the kimchi reaches your preferred flavor. Store the finished kimchi in a glass container with a nonreactive lid in the refrigerator. As long as it stays submerged in its brine, it will keep for months.

Ingredient Tip: If you find gochugaru (Korean red pepper flakes; see Tip, page 93), replace the fresh chile with ¼ cup of these mild dried peppers. For a sweeter ferment, add 1 teaspoon more of sugar.

Cultured Curtido (Cabbage Slaw)

Makes 1 half-gallon   **Prep time:** 15 minutes, plus 1 hour salting time   **Curing time:** 3 to 10 days

BUMPER CROP

The flavors of Salvadoran vinegar-pickled *curtido* (Eight-Hour Curtido, page 35) work just as well in a ferment, where they take on a sour flavor rather than a tangy one and build a slew of probiotics, which are so beneficial for the digestive system. The flavors strengthen the longer the slaw sits in the refrigerator, so I keep the chile light; you can choose a spicier pepper for more heat.

1 small (2-pound) head green cabbage

2 medium red onions (1 pound), thinly sliced (about 3⅓ cups)

5 medium carrots (1 pound), shredded (2½ cups)

1 Fresno chile, cut into ¼-inch rings (3 tablespoons)

5½ tablespoons Diamond Crystal kosher salt, divided

3 tablespoons minced fresh oregano or 1 tablespoon crumbled dried oregano

Zest of 2 limes

1. Set aside the cabbage's loose outer leaves. Place the stem end on a cutting board. Use a sharp knife to cut the cabbage down to the stem in quarters, then cut out the pieces of solid core. Lay each wedge flat-side down on the cutting board and cut it into thin strips.

2. In a large, wide bowl, put about half of the cabbage, onions, carrots, and chile. Sprinkle and toss the mix with 3 tablespoons of salt. Add the remaining vegetables and 2½ tablespoons of salt and toss again. Let sit for about 1 hour, then mix in the oregano and lime zest, pressing and squeezing to release liquid.

3. In a clean ½-gallon jar or crock, firmly pack the vegetables and liquid. Cover the surface with a whole cabbage leaf, top with a weight, and cover the fermenting vessel, preferably with an air lock. Let sit in a dark, cool place to cure.

4. After 24 hours, check that the surface layer is still submerged. If it's exposed, add enough brine with a 2.5% concentration (see the Brine Concentration chart on page 12) to submerge the vegetables. Continue to check the fermentation daily, releasing air bubbles over the first 2 days. Top off with brine and skim off any filmy surface layer as needed.

5. Taste after 3 to 5 days of curing; continue fermenting for an additional 3 to 5 days as needed, until the curtido reaches your preferred flavor. Store the finished curtido in a glass container with a nonreactive lid in the refrigerator. As long as it stays submerged in its brine, it will keep for months.

Smoky Full-Sour Pickles

Makes 1 half-gallon   **Prep time:** 15 minutes   **Curing time:** 1 to 4 weeks

BUMPER CROP

Full-sour pickles develop their flavor from a heavy hand with the salt and long, slow fermentation. Drawing inspiration from Linda Ziedrich's *The Joy of Pickling*, I developed this recipe using moderately smoky Russian Caravan tea from the Lake Missoula Tea Company and home-smoked chiles. For an even smokier flavor, swap in Lapsang souchong and replace the horseradish leaf with a handful of black currant leaves.

2 pounds 3- to 6-inch pickling cucumbers

1 quart unchlorinated water

6 tablespoons Diamond Crystal kosher salt

1 to 2 fresh horseradish or grape leaves (optional)

1 garlic head, separated into cloves

1 tablespoon coriander seeds

2 teaspoons smoky tea leaves, such as Russian Caravan or Lapsang souchong

½ teaspoon mustard seeds

1 teaspoon Szechuan peppercorns

1 dried chipotle pepper or other smoked chile, crumbled (optional)

1. Cut off a thin slice from the blossom end of each cucumber (see Tip, page 57), and then thoroughly chill the cucumbers in the refrigerator.

2. In a large measuring cup, whisk together the water and salt, stirring until the salt dissolves.

3. Line the bottom of a clean ½ gallon jar or crock with the horseradish leaves (if using). Add the peeled garlic cloves, coriander seeds, tea leaves, mustard seeds, peppercorns, and chile (if using). Add the cucumbers, packing them vertically and firmly but without bruising, up to the shoulder of the container. Pour in the brine, submerging the cucumbers; store extra brine in a small lidded jar. Top the cucumbers with a weight if needed and cover the fermenting vessel, preferably with an air lock. Let sit in a dark, cool place to cure.

4. After 24 hours, start to check the fermentation daily, ensuring the pickles are submerged and skimming off any filmy surface layer. If they're exposed, add enough brine with a 5% concentration (see the Brine Concentration chart on page 12) to submerge the cucumbers.

5. Taste after 1 week of curing; continue fermenting for an additional 3 weeks as needed, until the pickles reach your preferred flavor. Store the finished pickles in a glass container with a nonreactive lid in the refrigerator. As long as they stay submerged in their brine, they will keep for months.

Ingredient Tip: Cutting the blossom end off cucumbers (see Tip, page 57), chilling, and adding tannin-laden horseradish or grape leaves all improve cucumber pickle crispness (see "Varieties for Pickling," page 15). But the best way to get crunchy pickles is to start with ultra-fresh pickling cucumbers.

Switch Things Up: Dried chipotle chiles may be harder to find than powdered smoked paprika, but specialty stores and spice shops often carry them. For a substitution, choose non-smoked red pepper flakes instead of a smoked powder.

Half-Sour Dill Pickles

Makes 1 half-gallon   **Prep time:** 15 minutes   **Curing time:** 1 to 4 weeks

BUMPER CROP

Less salty than full sours, half-sour pickles are infused with the classic dill flavor. For extra heat and flavor, add a fresh chile and a dill head. The longer these pickles ferment, the better they taste. To check for full fermentation, slice into a pickle; it should be uniform in color, crunchy, and full of flavor.

2 pounds 3- to 6-inch pickling cucumbers

4 cups unchlorinated water

¼ cup Diamond Crystal kosher salt

1 or more fresh horseradish or grape leaves (optional)

4 garlic cloves

1 red jalapeño pepper, halved lengthwise (optional)

1 fresh dill head (optional)

1 tablespoon Basic Dilly Spice Blend (page 16)

1. Cut off a thin slice from the blossom end of each cucumber (see Tip, page 57), and then thoroughly chill the cucumbers in the refrigerator.

2. In a large measuring cup, whisk together the water and salt, stirring until the salt dissolves.

3. Line the bottom of a clean ½-gallon jar or crock with the horseradish leaves (if using). Add the garlic, pepper, dill head (if using), and spice blend. Add the cucumbers, packing them vertically and firmly but without bruising, up to the shoulder of the container. Pour in the brine, submerging the cucumbers; store extra brine in a small lidded jar. Top the cucumbers with a weight if needed and cover the fermenting vessel, preferably with an air lock. Let sit in a dark, cool place to cure.

4. After 24 hours, start to check the fermentation daily, ensuring the pickles are submerged and skimming off any filmy surface layer. If they're exposed, add enough brine with a 3.5% concentration (see the Brine Concentration chart on page 12) to submerge the cucumbers.

5. Taste after 1 week of curing; continue fermenting for an additional 3 weeks as needed, until the pickles reach your preferred flavor. Store the finished pickles in a glass container with a nonreactive lid in the refrigerator. As long as they stay submerged in their brine, they will keep for at least 6 months.

Don't Forget: The brine prevents spoilage, so the cucumbers must remain submerged throughout the fermentation process. If they start to float, add a weight.

Asparagus with Ginger

Makes 1 (24-ounce) jar　　　**Prep time:** 15 minutes　　　**Curing time:** 1 to 3 weeks

My asparagus pickling progression goes like this: The first harvest becomes Spring Asparagus (page 31) with spring garlic. Once this season's garlic scapes appear, the next rounds become Refrigerated Asparagus Spears (page 61). Finally, as asparagus production slows, the first bulb onions are big enough to use in fermented jars. I stuff a couple of onion tops, using the white "neck" between the bulb and the green leaves, in each jar. It's a delicious progression.

1 (2-inch) piece peeled fresh ginger, thinly sliced

15 small asparagus spears (8 ounces)

2 bulb onion tops, white parts only, or 6 scallions, white parts only (2 ounces)

2 cups unchlorinated water

2 tablespoons Diamond Crystal kosher salt

1. In a clean, tall 24-ounce jar, place the ginger slices. Cut the asparagus spears so that they are about 1¾ inches shorter than the jar rim, then tightly pack them into the jar. Slide the onions, cut to the same length as the asparagus, into the jar as you pack the spears.

2. In a large measuring cup, whisk together the water and salt, stirring until the salt dissolves. Pour the brine into the jar, submerging the asparagus spears but leaving about 1½ inches of headspace; store extra brine in a small lidded jar. Top the vegetables with a weight if needed and cover the fermenting vessel, preferably with an air lock. Let sit in a dark, cool place to cure.

3. After 24 hours, start to check the fermentation daily, ensuring the pickles are submerged and skimming off any filmy surface layer. If they're exposed, add enough brine with a 3.5% concentration (see the Brine Concentration chart on page 12) to submerge the asparagus.

4. Taste after 1 week of curing; continue fermenting for an additional 1 to 2 weeks as needed, until the asparagus reaches your preferred flavor. Store the finished asparagus in its jar with a nonreactive lid in the refrigerator. As long as it stays submerged in its brine, it will keep for months.

Ingredient Tip: Make these pickles earlier in the season with 1 bunch of spring onions or throughout the season with scallions. The flavor will grow stronger in the refrigerator, so pull and eat the onions early if you plan on storing the pickles more than a couple of weeks.

Chinese-Inspired Brined Beans

Makes 1 half-gallon   **Prep time:** 15 minutes   **Curing time:** 10 days
to 2 weeks

The first time I brined snap beans, every bite reminded me of sweet-and-sour bean dishes from childhood visits to Chinese restaurants. The lacto-fermentation gives a distinctly different flavor from vinegar-brined beans. If you live in a warm climate, try yard-long beans, sometimes called asparagus beans or Chinese long beans.

6 cups unchlorinated water

6 tablespoons Diamond
Crystal kosher salt

3 garlic cloves, smashed

2 dried Chinese red peppers
or other hot chiles, crumbled

½ teaspoon cumin seeds

6 black peppercorns, crushed

1½ pounds green and/or
yellow snap beans or
yard-long beans, ends
snapped off (6 cups)

1. In a large measuring cup, whisk together the water and salt, stirring until the salt dissolves.

2. In the bottom of a clean ½-gallon jar or crock, place the garlic, chiles, cumin, and peppercorns. Add the whole beans, packing them firmly but without bruising, up to the shoulder of the container. Pour in the brine, submerging the beans; store extra brine in a small lidded jar. Top the beans with a weight if needed and cover the fermenting vessel, preferably with an air lock. Let sit in a dark, cool place to cure.

3. After 24 hours, start to check the fermentation daily, ensuring the pickles are submerged and skimming off any filmy surface layer. If they're exposed, add enough brine with a 3.5% concentration (see the Brine Concentration chart on page 12) to submerge the beans.

4. Taste after 5 to 7 days of curing; continue fermenting for an additional 5 to 7 days as needed, until the pickles reach your preferred flavor. Store the finished beans in a glass container with a nonreactive lid in the refrigerator. As long as they stay submerged in their brine, they will keep for months.

Vietnamese Bean Sprouts

Makes 1 quart   **Prep time:** 10 minutes, plus   **Curing time:** 3 to 5 days
                                  2 hours sitting time

I grow sprouts in jars in my kitchen, particularly in winter, and knew mung bean sprouts would be good candidates for fermenting when I stored the leftover sprouts in a jar of water in the refrigerator: Even without salt, they wanted to bubble and ferment. Plus, they are a great plant-based source of protein and fiber.

8 ounces mung bean sprouts (2½ cups)

2 cups unchlorinated water

4 teaspoons Diamond Crystal kosher salt

¼ teaspoon sugar

2 garlic cloves, thinly sliced

1 dried Thai chile or other hot chile

1. Rinse the bean sprouts in a colander under cool running water and set aside to drain. In a medium measuring cup, whisk together the water, salt, and sugar, stirring until the salt and sugar dissolve.

2. In a clean quart jar, place the garlic and chile. Add the sprouts, packing them firmly but without crushing, up to the shoulder of the container. Pour in the brine and let sit for 2 hours; if the sprouts are not still submerged, cover the surface with cheesecloth before covering the fermenting vessel, preferably with an air lock. Let sit in a dark, cool place to cure.

3. After 24 hours, start to check the fermentation daily, ensuring the pickles are submerged and skimming off any filmy surface layer. If they're exposed, add a light weight that keeps them whole but submerged.

4. Taste after 2 days of curing; continue fermenting for an additional 1 to 3 days as needed, until the sprouts reach your preferred flavor. Store the pickled sprouts in their jar with a nonreactive lid in the refrigerator. As long as they stay submerged in their brine, they will keep for weeks.

Try It With: In Vietnam, the bean sprouts are often pickled with carrot and chives (*dua gia*). I like to pickle just the sprouts so that they can also be fried with garlic or tossed into pad thai, hot-and-sour soup, or stir-fry.

Shaved and Fermented Carrots

Makes 1 quart   **Prep time:** 15 minutes, plus 30 minutes salting time   **Curing time:** 24 hours

This is one of my favorite recipes for first-time fermenters: You get to practice basic techniques but eat the results quickly. You can include the peels of organic home-grown carrots in the jars; the bacteria found in the skins will aid the fermentation. Set aside the green, feathery tops for a tasty Carrot-Top Greens and Mint Salsa (page 140).

1¾ pounds carrots (4 cups)

2 tablespoons Diamond Crystal kosher salt

2 tablespoons sugar

2 tablespoons prepared horseradish or Vinegar-Based Horseradish Paste (page 150)

1 tablespoon peeled, minced fresh ginger

1 tablespoon coriander seeds, crushed

6 dried chiles de árbol or other small hot chiles, crumbled, or 1 tablespoon red pepper flakes

1. Using a vegetable peeler, peel off wide ribbons of carrot until you can no longer hold on to the core.

2. In a medium bowl, toss the peelings with salt and sugar. Add the horseradish paste, ginger, coriander seeds, and chiles and toss again, distributing the seasonings evenly.

3. Fill a second bowl partway with water and set the bowl evenly on the carrots, weighing them down. Let sit for about 30 minutes, until the carrots release liquid.

4. In a clean quart jar, firmly pack the carrots and liquid. Screw a nonreactive lid on the jar and store in the refrigerator for at least 24 hours before eating. For longer storage, add a weight to the jar so that the carrots are covered with liquid. As long as the carrots stay submerged in their brine, they will keep for weeks in the refrigerator.

Don't Forget: If you use your hands to toss and pack the vegetables, you probably want to wear rubber gloves; both fresh horseradish and dried chiles can irritate skin.

Preserved Lemons

Makes 1 quart   **Prep time:** 10 minutes   **Curing time:** 4 weeks

(BUMPER CROP)

I first tasted preserved lemons in Morocco without recognizing the zesty, salty, julienned bits as lemon peel. When I returned home and attempted to re-create the tagines and stews I'd enjoyed in family homes, the flavors were off until I learned about preserved lemons. Now I reach simultaneously for salt-mellowed lemons and brined green olives for many dishes. To make your own, choose organic lemons without waxed skin.

4 medium lemons (1 pound)

¾ cup Diamond Crystal kosher salt

Juice of 1 or 2 lemons (see Tip, page 43)

1. Cut each lemon lengthwise into quarters. In a medium bowl, toss the wedges and salt, coating every edge.

2. In a clean quart jar, scoop some salt, then add the lemons, packing them firmly so that they are wedged below the shoulder of the container. Scrape in the remaining salt, then add the juice of 1 lemon. Cover the jar with a nonreactive lid, and let sit in a dark, cool place.

3. Shake the jar daily for 5 to 7 days, redistributing the salt and accumulating juice. If the lemons are still exposed after 4 days, press them down firmly, releasing more liquid, then add the juice of another lemon as needed to cover the quarters. Once the lemon quarters stay fully covered, store in the refrigerator for at least 3 weeks before using. As long as the lemons stay submerged, they will keep for up to 6 months in the refrigerator.

Ingredient Tip: Room-temperature lemons unleash their juice more readily than chilled ones. Cut the lemons for juicing lengthwise so the halves will release the maximum liquid when you press and rotate the tines of a fork deeply in their center.

Try It With: To use preserved lemon, rinse off the salt and cut the skin into julienned pieces; some cooks use the pulp, too. Add it to tagines and other traditional North African dishes, sprinkle it on grilled fish or vegetables, or stir it into tomato or potato salad.

Dilly and Mustardy Kohlrabi Pickles

Makes 1 half-gallon   **Prep time:** 15 minutes   **Curing time:** 1 to 2 weeks

Kohlrabi takes the top prize in a funny-looking vegetable contest. It looks like a root, but its round green or purple bulb actually grows aboveground, with stems and leaves poking out at all angles, like a Hollywood alien. Look for full, unwilted leaves when buying kohlrabi; they indicate it was freshly picked and are delicious in salads and stir-fries.

2½ pounds kohlrabi

4 cups unchlorinated water

6 tablespoons Diamond Crystal kosher salt

2 tablespoons peeled and coarsely chopped horseradish root

4 teaspoons yellow mustard seeds

1½ teaspoons celery seeds

2 fresh dill heads or 4 teaspoons dill seeds

1 small onion, thinly sliced (1 cup)

1. Cut off the kohlrabi leaves, reserving them for another use, then cut the remaining stalks into 3-inch lengths. Peel the bulbs, then cut them into 3-inch-long, ½-inch-wide spears.

2. In a large measuring cup, whisk together the water and salt, stirring until the salt dissolves.

3. In the bottom of a clean ½-gallon jar or crock, place the horseradish root, mustard seeds, celery seeds, and dill heads. Add the kohlrabi stalks and spears and onion slices, packing them firmly but without bruising, up to the shoulder of the container. Pour in the brine, submerging the pieces; store extra brine in a small lidded jar. Cover the surface with a whole kohlrabi leaf, top with a weight if needed, and cover the fermenting vessel, preferably with an air lock. Let sit in a dark, cool place to cure.

4. After 24 hours, start to check the fermentation daily, ensuring the pickles are submerged and skimming off any filmy surface layer. If they're exposed, add enough brine with a 5% concentration (see the Brine Concentration chart on page 12) to submerge the kohlrabi.

5. Taste after 1 week of curing; continue fermenting for an additional week as needed, until the pickles reach your preferred flavor. Store the finished pickles in a glass container with a nonreactive lid in the refrigerator. As long as they stay submerged in their brine, they will keep for months.

Ingredient Tip: Young, small kohlrabi bulbs may be easy to peel with a vegetable peeler, but larger ones may have thick skin that requires a knife. Older kohlrabi may have tough stalks that will be woody when fermented; replace these with extra bulbs.

Spiced Fermented Pearl Onions

Makes 1 quart   **Prep time:** 20 minutes   **Curing time:** 2 to 4 weeks

If you've tried and loved Cocktail Onions (page 74), just wait until you taste this fermented version. They're worth the wait. The salty, sour tang gives a dimension to your beverages that even homemade vinegar-brined onions can't match. They also work beautifully on a cheese tray or atop pizza or grilled cheese toasts.

20 ounces fresh pearl onions
(4 cups)

4 cups boiling water

2 cups unchlorinated
cool water

2 tablespoons Diamond
Crystal kosher salt

2 teaspoons Sweet-Savory
Spice Blend (page 16)

1 tablespoon fresh tarragon or
1 teaspoon dried tarragon

2 bay leaves

1. Put the onions in a medium heatproof bowl and pour in the boiling water. Let sit for 1 minute, then drain the onions and plunge them immediately into a bowl of cold water. Cut off the root and top tips with a sharp knife, then slip off the outer skins.

2. In a small measuring cup, whisk together the cool water and salt, stirring until the salt dissolves.

3. In the bottom of a clean quart jar, put the spice blend and tarragon. Add the onions, packing them firmly but without bruising and sliding in the bay leaves, up to the shoulder of the container. Pour in the brine, submerging the onions; store extra brine in a small lidded jar. Top the onions with a weight if needed and cover the fermenting vessel, preferably with an air lock. Let sit in a dark, cool place to cure.

4. After 24 hours, start to check the fermentation daily, ensuring the pickles are submerged and skimming off any filmy surface layer. If they're exposed, add enough brine with a 3.5% concentration (see the Brine Concentration chart on page 12) to submerge the onions.

5. Taste after 2 weeks of curing; continue fermenting for an additional 1 to 2 weeks as needed, until the onions reach your preferred flavor. Store the finished pickles in their jar with a nonreactive lid in the refrigerator. As long as they stay submerged in their brine, they will keep for months.

Ingredient Tip: Although you can use pre-peeled frozen pearl onions in this recipe, they soften significantly as they ferment, losing their crunchy texture. I consider the few extra minutes of peeling to be time well spent. Produce departments typically offer mesh bags of fresh pearl onions.

Fermented Red Onions

Makes 1 quart   **Prep time:** 15 minutes, plus 30 minutes salting time   **Curing time:** 4 to 6 weeks

Onions hold so much liquid in their fleshy layers that they quickly become a lively, bubbly ferment. For added fun, choose red onions and use a beet half as an additional weight. As the onions ferment, the beet will release its color down into the jar, turning the contents a brilliant pink. For a less colorful jar, choose white or yellow onions and skip the beet.

2 medium red onions (1 pound), cut in ¼-inch rings (3⅓ cups)

4 teaspoons Diamond Crystal kosher salt

1 garlic clove, minced

1 dried Japones chile or other hot chile, crumbled

½ teaspoon black peppercorns

½ raw red beet, scrubbed and with top removed

1. In a medium mixing bowl, layer the onions with salt. Add the garlic, chile, and peppercorns and toss to combine.

2. Fill a second bowl partway with water and set it evenly on the onions, weighing them down. Let sit for about 30 minutes, until the onions release liquid.

3. In a clean quart jar, firmly pack the onions and liquid. Top with the beet half and a weight, then cover the fermenting vessel, preferably with an air lock. Let sit in a dark, cool place to cure.

4. After 24 hours, check that the surface layer is submerged. If it's exposed, add enough brine with a 2.5% concentration (see the Brine Concentration chart on page 12) to submerge the onions. Continue to check the fermentation daily, releasing air bubbles over the first 3 days. Top off with brine and skim off any filmy surface layer as needed.

5. Taste after 4 weeks of curing; you can continue fermenting for an additional 2 weeks, until the onions reach your preferred flavor. Remove the beet; stir the onions to evenly distribute the color. Store the finished pickles in their jar with a nonreactive lid in the refrigerator. As long as they stay submerged in their brine, they will keep at least 6 months.

Beer-Pickled Jalapeños

Makes 1 quart

Prep time: 10 minutes, plus 30 minutes cooling time

Curing time: 1 to 2 weeks at room temperature, plus 1 week refrigerated

As soon as I spotted a recipe for beer-fermented pickles, I knew I had to try this brine. The idea of beer-infused jalapeños sliced onto a homemade veggie burger and served with a pint of rye IPA turned into a killer meal. Save the hoppy brews for drinking: These pickles work best with less bitter, less alcoholic beers.

20 medium jalapeño peppers (12 ounces)

1¼ cups low-IBU and low-ABV beer, such as a blonde or brown ale

1¼ cups unchlorinated water

2½ tablespoons Diamond Crystal kosher salt

2 tablespoons sugar (optional)

¼ teaspoon black peppercorns

⅛ teaspoon yellow mustard seeds

2 garlic cloves, smashed

1. Using a sharp knife, poke 1 or 2 holes in each pepper (wear gloves when handling the peppers if your skin is easily irritated).

2. In a small saucepan, bring the beer, water, salt, and sugar (if using) to a simmer, stirring to dissolve the salt and sugar. Remove the pan from the heat and add the peppercorns and mustard seeds; let the brine infuse for about 30 minutes, until it has cooled to room temperature.

3. Put the garlic in the bottom of a clean quart jar. Add the jalapeños, packing them firmly but without bruising, up to the shoulder of the container. Ladle in the brine, submerging the jalapeños; store extra brine in a small lidded jar. Top the jalapeños with a weight if needed, and cover the fermenting vessel, preferably with an air lock. Let sit in a dark, cool place to cure.

4. After 24 hours, start to check the fermentation daily, ensuring the pickles are submerged and skimming off any filmy surface layer. If they're exposed, add enough brine with a 3.5% concentration (see the Brine Concentration chart on page 12) to submerge the jalapeños.

5. Taste after 1 week of curing; continue fermenting for an additional week as needed, until the chiles reach your preferred flavor. Store the finished peppers in their jar with a nonreactive lid in the refrigerator for at least 1 week before eating. As long as they stay submerged in their brine, they will keep for weeks.

Salt-Brined Peppers

Makes 1 quart   **Prep time:** 15 minutes   **Curing time:** 3 to 4 weeks

Peter Piper may have loved these pickled peppers, but he'd have needed 8 batches to pick a peck. I recommend sticking to a quart jar, starting a new jar around the time you put the finished ferment in the refrigerator, for a steady supply all season. The peppers will soften the longer you store them. Any variety works, from mini sweet lunchbox peppers to spicy cherry bombs; I typically mix heat levels so that the jar fulfills every use and taste. Rubber gloves keep chile oils from irritating your skin as you work; a narrow-mouth jar can help submerge the peppers.

1 pound mixed hot and
  mild peppers
2 cups unchlorinated water
2½ tablespoons Diamond
  Crystal kosher salt

1. Using a sharp knife, remove the stems and cut the peppers in half; leave the seeds and membranes if you want a hotter brine. In a large measuring cup, whisk together the water and salt, stirring until the salt dissolves.

2. Fill a clean quart jar with peppers, packing them firmly but without bruising, up to the shoulder of the container. Pour in the brine, submerging the vegetables; store extra brine in a small lidded jar. Top the peppers with a weight if needed, and cover the fermenting vessel, preferably with an air lock. Let sit in a dark, cool place to cure.

3. After 24 hours, start to check the fermentation daily, ensuring the pickles are submerged and skimming off any filmy surface layer. If they're exposed, add enough brine with a 4.25% concentration (see the Brine Concentration chart on page 12) to submerge the peppers.

4. Taste after 2 weeks of curing; continue fermenting an additional 1 to 2 weeks as needed, until the peppers reach your preferred flavor. Store the finished peppers in their jar with a nonreactive lid in the refrigerator. As long as they stay submerged in their brine, they will keep for a couple of months.

Try It With: To keep their probiotic goodness, try these peppers blended into hummus or pureed with fresh tomatoes and vegetable broth to start a gazpacho, or place them uncooked atop salad or pizza. For a more flavorful brine, add a tablespoon of Ultra Pickling Spice Blend (page 16).

Salad Radish Slices

Makes 1 quart   **Prep time:** 15 minutes   **Curing time:** 4 to 7 days

BUMPER CROP

A short, weeklong ferment of round salad radishes brings out their natural spicy-sweet flavor. Choose all-red varieties or multicolored mixes. You can also try long red French breakfast radishes, sweet purple Polish radishes, and spicy golden Czech radishes. Darker-skinned varieties will tinge the brine pink.

1 cup unchlorinated water

1½ tablespoons Diamond Crystal kosher salt

1 teaspoon mustard seeds

½ teaspoon black peppercorns

1 bay leaf

24 salad radishes, cut into ¼-inch-thick rounds (2 cups)

1. In a small measuring cup, whisk together the water and salt, stirring until the salt dissolves.

2. In the bottom of a clean quart jar, place the mustard seeds, peppercorns, and bay leaf. Add the radish slices, packing them firmly but without bruising, up to the shoulder of the container. Pour in the brine, submerging the vegetables; store extra brine in a small lidded jar. Top the radishes with a weight if needed and cover the fermenting vessel, preferably with an air lock. Let sit in a dark, cool place to cure.

3. After 24 hours, start to check the fermentation daily, ensuring the pickles are submerged and skimming off any filmy surface layer. If they're exposed, add enough brine with a 5% concentration (see the Brine Concentration chart on page 12) to submerge the radishes.

4. Taste after 4 days of curing; continue fermenting for an additional 1 to 3 days as needed, until the radishes reach your preferred flavor. Store the finished pickles in their jar with a nonreactive lid in the refrigerator. As long as they stay submerged in their brine, they will keep for weeks.

Short-Ferment Potatoes

Makes 1 half-gallon   **Prep time:** 15 minutes   **Curing time:** 5 to 10 days
Cook time: 50 minutes

This recipe isn't really about preservation; it's about the perfect home-roasted potato. The salt brine works as in any fermentation. It draws water from the potatoes, replacing it with the brining solution and adding flavor. When roasted at fairly high heat for nearly an hour, brined potatoes develop a crackly exterior and creamy center. They're so flavorful you'll be able to skip the condiments when serving.

3¼ cups unchlorinated water

¼ cup Diamond Crystal kosher salt

2 peeled garlic cloves

2¾ pounds unpeeled potatoes, cut into 1½-inch pieces (7 cups)

Olive oil, for roasting

1. In a large measuring cup, whisk together the water and salt, stirring until the salt dissolves.

2. In the bottom of a clean ½-gallon jar or crock, place the garlic cloves. Add the potatoes, packing them firmly but without bruising, up to the shoulder of the container. Pour in the brine, submerging the potatoes; store extra brine in a small lidded jar. Top the potatoes with a weight if needed and cover the fermenting vessel with an air lock. Let sit in a dark, cool place to cure.

3. After 24 hours, start to check the fermentation daily for 5 days for slightly crisp, tangy potatoes and up to 10 days for crackly, salty, sour potatoes. Make sure the vegetables stay submerged and skim off any filmy surface layer as needed. If they're exposed, add enough brine with a 4.25% concentration (see the Brine Concentration chart on page 12) to submerge the potatoes.

4. To use, remove the potatoes with a slotted spoon and let drain completely. Preheat the oven to 450°F. Lightly coat a large rimmed baking sheet with olive oil.

5. Put the potatoes in the pan and drizzle with olive oil. Toss to coat, then spread out the potatoes in a single layer. Roast for about 45 minutes, stirring the potatoes halfway through the cooking time, until cooked through and lightly browned.

6. Serve immediately. If you didn't cook the entire jar, any remaining potatoes can be stored in the refrigerator, submerged in their brine, for a few days; they'll continue to sour slowly. Leftover cooked potatoes will lose their crispness if not eaten immediately but can be refrigerated for a couple of days.

Ingredient Tip: Different potato varieties may brown more slowly or more quickly with a different texture in the interior. For example, russet potatoes will have fluffier centers, while a Red Norland will be creamier inside. But any variety will work for this recipe.

Switch It Up: The fermented garlic cloves will be as tangy as the potatoes and can be cooked, too; just add them during the last 10 minutes of cooking time to keep them from burning. For bonus garlic flavor, add a few fresh unpeeled cloves at the same time; they'll become soft and gooey inside their skins.

Sambal Oelek (Chile Paste), page 132

Relish, Hot Sauce, and Other Condiments

Dill Cucumber Relish

Makes 7 half-pints

Prep time: 25 minutes, plus 2 hours salting and 12 to 18 hours infusing time

Cook time: 5 minutes
Processing time: 10 minutes
Curing time: 24 hours

CAN THIS   **BUMPER CROP**

Misshapen, blemished, or oversized cucumbers can be ugly or soften quickly as a jar of pickles, but get a second life in relish. I often set aside unsightly vegetables for relish while I'm processing other pickles. The US Department of Agriculture says pickle relish can be processed for the same time in ½ pints or pints; just double the recipe for a full batch of the larger jars.

2 pounds pickling cucumbers, diced (4 cups)

1 pound onion, diced (2 cups)

½ large green bell pepper, diced (½ cup)

2½ tablespoons Morton pickling salt

Ice cubes

5 teaspoons Ultra Pickling Spice Blend (page 16)

2¼ cups apple cider vinegar (5% acidity)

2 tablespoons sugar

¼ cup finely chopped fresh dill or 4 teaspoons dried dill

1. In a large bowl, combine the diced cucumbers, onion, and bell pepper, sprinkle with salt, and stir. Cover with ice cubes and a dish towel and let sit at room temperature for 2 hours.

2. Drain the vegetables in a fine-mesh colander; rinse them under cool running water, then drain again and return the vegetables to the bowl.

3. Tie the spice blend into a cheesecloth bag and place it in a large saucepan. Add the vinegar and sugar and bring to a boil, stirring to dissolve the sugar. Ladle the brine over the vegetables; stir in the dill. Transfer the spice sack to the bowl. Cover the bowl, let the relish cool to room temperature, then refrigerate for 12 to 18 hours.

4. In a wide 6- to 8-quart pot, bring the relish to a boil, then remove the spice bag. Ladle the relish into clean, hot ½-pint jars; leave ½ inch of headspace. Remove any air bubbles with a bamboo or wooden chopstick and wipe each jar's rim. Cap the jars with two-piece canning lids.

5. Process the relish in a boiling-water bath for 10 minutes, plus your altitude adjustment (see page 191). Store the jars in a dry, dark, cool place for at least 24 hours before eating. The relish is best eaten within a year.

Ingredient Tip: Relish texture is a personal preference. My food processor quickly turns the vegetables into tiny bits. If you like chunky relish, it might be worth dicing with a knife. The processor's shredding disk or a large-hole cheese grater gives yet another, softer texture.

Sweetened Cucumber Relish

Makes 7 half-pints

Prep time: 25 minutes, plus 2 hours salting and 12 to 18 hours infusing time

Cook time: 5 minutes
Processing time: 10 minutes
Curing time: 24 hours

CAN THIS **BUMPER CROP**

I updated this classic from my mom's old copy of the *Ball Blue Book: The Guide to Home Canning and Freezing*. This version dials back the sugar to suit today's taste buds and tweaks the produce-to-vinegar ratio to match current pH guidelines from the US Food and Drug Administration and National Center for Home Food Preservation.

2 pounds pickling cucumbers, diced (4 cups)

1 pound bell peppers, diced (2 cups)

1 medium onion, minced (½ cup)

2½ tablespoons Morton pickling salt

1½ teaspoons ground turmeric

Ice cubes

1½ teaspoons mustard seeds

1 teaspoon Sweet-Savory Spice Blend (page 16)

2¼ cups apple cider vinegar (5% acidity)

⅔ cup brown sugar

1. In a large bowl, combine the cucumbers, bell peppers, and onion, sprinkle with salt and turmeric, and stir. Cover with ice cubes and a dish towel and let sit at room temperature for 2 hours.

2. Drain the vegetables in a fine-mesh colander; rinse them under cool running water, then drain again and return the vegetables to the bowl.

3. Tie the mustard seeds and spice blend into a cheesecloth bag and place it in a large saucepan. Add the vinegar and sugar and bring to a boil, stirring to dissolve the sugar. Ladle the brine over the vegetables. Transfer the spice sack to the bowl. Cover the bowl, let the relish cool to room temperature, about 30 minutes, then refrigerate for 12 to 18 hours.

4. In a wide 6- to 8-quart pot, bring the relish to a boil, then remove the spice bag. Ladle the relish into seven clean, hot ½-pint jars; leave ½ inch of headspace. Remove any air bubbles with a bamboo or wooden chopstick and wipe each jar's rim. Cap the jars with two-piece canning lids.

5. Process the relish in a boiling-water bath for 10 minutes, plus your altitude adjustment (see page 191). Store the jars in a dry, dark, cool place for at least 24 hours before eating. The relish is best eaten within a year.

Zucchini Relish

Makes 7 half-pints

Prep time: 30 minutes, plus 2 hours salting time
Cook time: 15 minutes

Processing time: 15 minutes
Curing time: 24 hours

CAN THIS

In the 1970s, my great-aunt gave my mom this classic recipe, and it's stood the test of time. I've made only minor tweaks to match today's safe-canning standards. The original recipe called for ground vegetables, and I imagine my great-aunt used an old-fashioned meat grinder—and probably was in tears by the time she finished the onions. For a fine yet less tearful texture, shred and chop in a food processor.

5 medium zucchini (1¾ pounds), shredded (4 cups)

2 medium onions, shredded (1½ cups)

5 teaspoons Morton pickling salt

Ice cubes

2 medium bell peppers, diced (1½ cups)

2 jalapeño peppers or 1 Fresno chile, minced (3 tablespoons)

1¾ cups apple cider vinegar (5% acidity)

¾ cup sugar

½ teaspoon ground nutmeg

½ teaspoon celery seeds

½ teaspoon freshly ground black pepper

½ teaspoon turmeric

1. In a large bowl, combine the zucchini and onions, sprinkle with salt, and stir. Cover with ice cubes and a dish towel and let sit at room temperature for 2 hours.

2. Drain the vegetables in a fine-mesh colander; rinse them under cool running water, then drain again, squeezing out as much water as possible. Return the vegetables to the bowl, and mix in all the bell peppers and jalapeños.

3. In a wide 6- to 8-quart pot, bring the vinegar and sugar to a simmer; stir in the nutmeg, celery seeds, black pepper, and turmeric. Add the vegetables, bring the mixture to a boil, then lower the heat and simmer slowly for 15 minutes, until slightly thickened.

4. Return the relish to a boil. Ladle it into seven clean, hot ½-pint jars; leave ½ inch of headspace. Remove any air bubbles with a bamboo or wooden chopstick and wipe each jar's rim. Cap the jars with two-piece canning lids.

5. Process the relish in a boiling-water bath for 15 minutes, plus your altitude adjustment (see page 191). Store the jars in a dry, dark, cool place for at least 24 hours before eating. The relish is best eaten within a year.

Switch Things Up: Green zucchini and yellow summer squash can be safely used in this recipe, as can any variety of onion and any color or spiciness of chile. Choose vegetables in a mix of shades for the most colorful jars.

Grilled Onion Relish

Makes 7 half-pints

Prep time: 20 minutes
Cook time: 40 to 50 minutes

Processing time: 10 minutes
Curing time: 24 hours

CAN THIS **BUMPER CROP**

Grill-charred vegetables boost the flavor of this lightly sweetened relish. Crushing most of the whole spices makes them easier to eat while maximizing flavor, but leave the mustard seeds whole, because they will soften and pop in your mouth after the jars sit for a couple of weeks. For a smoother, milder relish, put the whole spices into a cheesecloth bag and remove it from the relish just before processing.

6 pounds red onions, halved crosswise

2 medium red bell peppers, halved lengthwise

2 teaspoons ground turmeric

2 teaspoons sweet smoked paprika

5 cups apple cider vinegar (5% acidity)

6 tablespoons sugar

3 tablespoons molasses

1 tablespoon Morton pickling salt

2 tablespoons yellow mustard seeds

4 teaspoons coriander seeds, crushed

4 peppercorns, crushed

2 dried chiles de árbol or other hot chiles, crumbled

1. Place the onions and peppers, cut-side down, directly on a medium-hot grill or on a baking sheet under an oven broiler set to high heat. Cook on the grill for 5 minutes, flip, and cook for another 3 to 5 minutes, until lightly charred and somewhat softened. If using the broiler, turn the vegetables more frequently, removing them from the oven when evenly charred. Let cool.

2. Dice the onions and peppers and put them in a large bowl. Sprinkle with the turmeric and paprika and stir to combine.

3. In a wide 6- to 8-quart pot, bring the vinegar, sugar, molasses, and salt to a simmer; stir in the mustard seeds, coriander seeds, peppercorns, and chiles. Add the vegetables, bring the mixture to a boil, then lower the heat and simmer slowly for 30 to 40 minutes, until the onion is firm but translucent.

4. Return the relish to a boil. Ladle it into seven clean, hot ½-pint jars; leave ½ inch of headspace. Remove any air bubbles with a bamboo or wooden chopstick and wipe each jar's rim. Cap the jars with two-piece canning lids.

5. Process the relish in a boiling-water bath for 10 minutes, plus your altitude adjustment (see page 191). Store the jars in a dry, dark, cool place for at least 24 hours before eating. The relish is best eaten within a year.

Fermented Red Hot Sauce

Makes 1 pint

Prep time: 30 minutes, plus 30 minutes cooling time
Cook time: 5 minutes

Curing time: 2 to 5 weeks fermenting, plus 2 days in the refrigerator

When I started fermenting hot sauces, I wanted a smoky flavor but quickly learned that even low-temperature home-smoking killed the *Lactobacillus* bacteria needed to successfully ferment peppers. I'd nearly given up the idea when I discovered that Fresno chiles, with a natural hint of smokiness in the peppers themselves, easily imparted their flavor into the sauce. By blending them with bell peppers, you end up with a medium-heat sauce that needs no added smokiness or sweetener.

1 large red bell pepper, seeded and coarsely chopped (1¼ cups)

14 Fresno chiles, seeded and coarsely chopped (1¼ cups)

2 tablespoons Diamond Crystal kosher salt

½ cup apple cider vinegar (5% acidity)

1. Wearing rubber gloves, in a medium bowl, mix together the chopped bell pepper and chiles. Sprinkle with the salt and mix again, evenly distributing the salt and pressing to release liquid.

2. In a clean pint jar, firmly pack the peppers and liquid; leave at least 1 inch of headspace. Cover the surface with cheesecloth, top with a weight, and cover the fermenting vessel, preferably with an air lock. Let sit in a dark, cool place to cure.

3. After 24 hours, check that the surface layer is submerged. If it's exposed, add enough brine with a 3.5% concentration (see the Brine Concentration chart on page 12) to submerge the peppers. Continue to check the fermentation daily, releasing air bubbles over the first 3 days. Top off the jar with brine and skim off any filmy surface layer as needed.

4. Taste after 2 to 3 weeks of curing; continue fermenting for an additional 1 to 2 weeks as needed, until the peppers reach your preferred flavor.

5. Pour the fermented peppers and their brine into a food processor or blender. Add the vinegar and puree until smooth. Transfer the hot sauce to a medium saucepan and bring it to a boil. Lower the heat to medium-low and simmer for 5 minutes. Remove from the heat and let sit for about 30 minutes, until it has cooled to room temperature. (Heating the sauce stops the fermentation and makes it easier to store.)

6. Insert a funnel into the top of a clean glass 16-ounce bottle or two 8-ounce bottles. Pour in the hot sauce; leave ½ inch of headspace. Cap with a nonreactive lid and refrigerate for at least 2 days before using. It will keep for months in the refrigerator.

Switch it Up: Add more vinegar for a thinner sauce, or pour off some of the brine and replace it with vinegar if the fermented peppers are too salty for your tastes. You can also strain the sauce, as directed for Scratch-Made Sriracha (page 130), for a thinner mixture.

Spicy Vinegar

Makes 1 pint   **Prep time:** 10 minutes   **Curing time:** 1 day

Some people pickle peppers to enjoy their crunch. Others infuse vinegar with heat to sprinkle it on dishes and into cocktails. Bottled spicy vinegar, called *pique*, replaces thicker hot sauce as a condiment in Puerto Rico, and a more watered-down version is popular in Hawaii, called chile pepper water. The spiciness is up to you: Choose hot or mild chiles, from habanero to aji, jalapeño, or Anaheim; sweeter peppers like a bell or Cubanelle variety; or a blend.

6 ounces mixed hot and mild peppers, stems removed

12 black peppercorns

2 garlic cloves, thinly sliced

1¼ cups apple cider or white wine vinegar (5% acidity)

1. With gloved hands, slice the peppers lengthwise in half or quarters so that they are small enough to feed through the neck of a clean glass 16-ounce bottle or two 8-ounce bottles. Scrape out the seeds if desired.

2. Place the peppercorns in the bottom of the bottle (evenly divide them and all other ingredients if using two bottles). Tip the bottle at a 45-degree angle, then add the peppers, a slice at a time, interspersing with the garlic.

3. Set the bottle upright, insert a small funnel, and pour in the vinegar to fill the container; leave ½ inch of headspace. Cap with a nonreactive lid, shake to distribute the flavors, and refrigerate for at least 1 day before using. It will keep for up to a year in the refrigerator.

Ingredient Tip: The real beauty of a bottle of multicolored peppers is that you can infuse vinegar with their flavor and eat them as pickles. Alternatively, you can top off the vinegar as it runs low, continuously transferring flavor to the brine and eventually using the softened peppers in soup or other cooked dishes.

Chile and Tomatillo Hot Sauce

Makes 12 ounces   **Prep time:** 10 minutes   **Curing time:** 4 days

One of my favorite local breweries, Bonsai Brewing Project, inspired this recipe with a similar house-made hot sauce it sells and keeps on the bar. This vinegar-based green hot sauce tastes milder than an all-pepper version, with a slight sweetness from the tomatillos. It's simple enough to make a bottle at a time but keeps long enough for larger batches.

7 medium jalapeño peppers, stemmed and halved lengthwise (1⅓ cups)

5 medium tomatillos, husked and halved (1¼ cups)

¼ small onion, chopped (2 tablespoons)

1 garlic clove, smashed

½ cup white wine vinegar (5% acidity)

½ teaspoon Morton pickling salt

1. Remove the seeds from the jalapeños, if desired. In a food processor, combine the jalapeños, tomatillos, onion, and garlic; process until minced. Add the vinegar and salt, then process until smooth, scraping down the food processor bowl as needed.

2. Insert a funnel into the top of a clean glass 12-ounce bottle. Pour in the hot sauce; leave ½ inch of head-space. Cap with a nonreactive lid and refrigerate for at least 4 days before using. It will keep for months in the refrigerator.

Switch it Up: For a tasty alternative, grill the vegetables before processing them, adding ¼ cup of water to make up for the liquid lost while cooking.

Scratch-Made Sriracha

Makes 1 pint

Prep time: 40 minutes, plus 10 minutes cooling time
Cook time: 5 minutes

Curing time: 2 to 5 weeks fermenting, plus 2 days in the refrigerator

Sriracha has become a household name, even if most of its Western fans don't know that the fermented garlic-chile paste is named for a coastal town in Thailand but was created by a Vietnamese immigrant to Los Angeles. The sauce itself is simple in its ingredients, and when you make it at home you can adjust the heat, garlic, and thickness as desired, and you avoid the preservatives.

2 pounds large red jalapeño peppers, stems removed (about 40)

4 to 6 garlic cloves

¼ cup Diamond Crystal kosher salt

3 tablespoons brown sugar

1 cup unseasoned rice vinegar (4.3% acidity)

1. In a food processor, coarsely chop the chiles, including the green tops and seeds, and the garlic. Add the salt and process until the vegetables are finely chopped and release liquid.

2. Wearing rubber gloves, firmly pack the vegetables and liquid into a clean quart jar; leave at least 1 inch of head-space. Cover the surface with cheesecloth, top with a weight, and cover the fermenting vessel, preferably with an air lock. Let sit in a dark, cool place to cure.

3. After 24 hours, check that the surface layer is submerged. If it's exposed, add enough brine with a 3.5% concentration to submerge the peppers. Continue to check the fermentation daily, releasing air bubbles over the first 3 days. Top off the jar with brine and skim off any filmy surface layer as needed.

4. Taste after 2 to 3 weeks of curing; continue fermenting for an additional 1 to 2 weeks as needed, until the peppers reach your preferred flavor.

5. Pour the fermented peppers into a medium saucepan, add the sugar and vinegar, then bring to a boil. Lower the heat to medium-low and simmer for 5 minutes. Remove from the heat and let sit for about 10 minutes, until cool enough to handle. Transfer the sauce to a food processor and puree until smooth.

6. Set a fine-mesh colander over a large measuring cup. Pour the sauce through the colander, pressing the mash to extract its liquid.

7. Insert a funnel into the top of a clean glass 16-ounce bottle or two 8-ounce bottles. Pour in the hot sauce; leave ½ inch of headspace. Cap with a nonreactive lid and refrigerate for at least 2 days before using. It will keep for months in the refrigerator.

Ingredient Tip: Chop the chiles with a knife and skip the final puree if you don't have a food processor. Wear rubber gloves throughout and expect less sauce after straining. The remaining mash can replace fresh chiles. Just keep it sealed in the refrigerator for up to a month or dehydrate it in a well-ventilated area for long-term storage.

Sambal Oelek (Chile Paste)

Makes 1 (4-ounce) jar   **Prep time:** 5 minutes

A sambal, or chile condiment, can be as simple as chiles and salt or can be expanded with other flavors, such as garlic, lime, and coconut. *Oelek* refers to grinding into paste. A staple in Southeast Asia, sambal oelek has become common on American grocery stores shelves thanks to California-based Huy Fong Foods and its flagship trio of hot sauces emblazoned with a proud rooster. At home, make it milder with jalapeños or fiery with serrano or even Thai chiles.

4 ounces red chiles, stemmed and halved

¾ teaspoon Diamond Crystal kosher salt

1½ teaspoons unseasoned rice vinegar (4.3% acidity)

1. Remove the seeds from the chiles, if desired. In a food processor, combine the chiles, salt, and vinegar, then pulse to form a coarse paste.

2. Use the paste immediately or pack it into a clean 4-ounce jar. Screw on a nonreactive lid and store in the refrigerator for weeks.

Don't Forget: Wear rubber gloves when handling chiles. Scrape out membranes and seeds with a grapefruit spoon or paring knife, or leave them in for a hotter paste. A food processor or blender makes quick work of the chiles. If you hold down the button too long, it will sometimes liquefy them.

Italian Plum and Apple Chutney

Makes 7 half-pints

Prep time: 20 minutes
Cook time: 30 minutes

Processing time: 10 minutes
Curing time: 24 hours

CAN THIS **BUMPER CROP**

This gorgeous chutney can be served as a spread, glaze, condiment, or sauce. I put it on everything, from breakfast sandwiches to pound cake. Oblong, purple Italian prune plums, sometimes called blue plums, aren't as juicy as a round plums. In chutney, the mouthfeel is more like a jam, with flecks of skin replacing the texture of raisins and other dried fruits often added to chutneys.

2½ pounds Italian prune plums, chopped (6 cups)

1 pound apples, chopped (2 cups)

1 medium onion, finely chopped (½ cup)

1 tablespoon peeled, minced fresh ginger

2 garlic cloves, minced

1½ cups sugar

1¼ cups apple cider vinegar (5% acidity)

2 teaspoons yellow mustard seeds

1 teaspoon Morton pickling salt

¼ teaspoon red pepper flakes

¼ cup bottled lemon juice (5% acidity)

2 tablespoons chopped fresh mint or 2 teaspoons crumbled dried mint

1. In a wide 8-quart or larger pot, combine the plums, apples, onion, ginger, and garlic. Stir in the sugar, vinegar, mustard seeds, salt, and red pepper flakes. Bring to a boil over medium heat, stirring often. Lower the heat to medium-low and boil gently, stirring occasionally, for about 30 minutes, until the onions are translucent and the mixture is thick enough to cling to a spoon. Remove from the heat and stir in the lemon juice and mint.

2. Ladle the hot chutney into seven clean, hot ½-pint jars; leave ½ inch of headspace. Remove any air bubbles with a bamboo or wooden chopstick and wipe each jar's rim. Cap the jars with two-piece canning lids.

3. Process in a boiling-water bath for 10 minutes, plus your altitude adjustment (see page 191). Store the jars in a dry, dark, cool place for at least 24 hours before eating. The chutney is best eaten within a year.

Switch Things Up: If you have different plums, you can still use them in this recipe in the same volume. But you may need to cook them longer; the juicier the plum, the longer it will take to thicken the chutney.

Green Tomato Chutney

Makes 7 half-pints

Prep time: 45 minutes, plus 6 hours salting time
Cook time: 45 minutes to 1 hour 15 minutes

Processing time: 10 minutes
Curing time: 24 hours

CAN THIS **BUMPER CROP**

Green tomatoes and apples combine into a sweet and tangy chutney. I make this late in the season, when a freeze threatens and I'm pulling boxes of green tomatoes off my plants. Many of these tomatoes will ripen surprisingly well in boxes indoors, but I pull out those with any damage and turn them straight into this chutney. Because apples are ripening in the orchard around the same time, they make a perfect seasonal pairing.

4 pounds green tomatoes, chopped (8 cups)

2 medium green bell peppers, chopped (1¾ cups)

1 medium onion, sliced (1½ cups)

¼ cup Morton pickling salt

Ice cubes

2 cups apple cider vinegar (5% acidity)

4 pounds apples, peeled, cored, and chopped (8 cups)

2 cups brown sugar

1 teaspoon mustard seeds

1 teaspoon coriander seeds

½ teaspoon Sweet-Savory Spice Blend (page 16)

2 pasilla chiles or hotter dried chiles, crumbled

2 garlic cloves, minced

2 teaspoons peeled, minced fresh ginger

1. In a large bowl, layer the tomatoes, bell peppers, and onion with the salt. Cover with ice cubes and a dish towel and refrigerate for 6 hours or overnight.

2. Drain the vegetables in a colander; rinse them under cool running water, then drain again.

3. Pour the vinegar into a wide 6- to 8-quart pot. Add the chopped apples to the vinegar, stirring often to coat the pieces. Add the drained vegetables. Bring to a boil over medium-high heat and cook, uncovered and stirring frequently, for 20 to 30 minutes, until the vegetables are soft. Add the sugar. Return to a boil, stirring to dissolve the sugar, then lower the heat to medium-low and boil gently, stirring often, for 15 to 25 minutes, until the chutney starts to thicken.

4. Tie the mustard seeds, coriander seeds, spice blend, and chiles into a cheesecloth bag. Add the spice bag, garlic, and ginger to the thickened chutney. Continue to boil gently and stir frequently for an additional 10 to 20 minutes, until the chutney is thick enough to cling to a spoon. Remove the spice bag.

5. Ladle the hot chutney into seven clean, hot ½-pint jars; leave ½ inch of headspace. Remove any air bubbles with a bamboo or wooden chopstick and wipe each jar's rim. Cap the jars with two-piece canning lids.

6. Process the chutney in a boiling-water bath for 10 minutes, plus your altitude adjustment (see page 191). Store the jars in a dry, dark, cool place for at least 24 hours before eating. The chutney is best eaten within a year.

Switch Things Up: You could skip the salting instructions, reducing the salt to 2 teaspoons and adding it to the vinegar. I use the technique for two reasons: It lets me split the process into stages, and drawing out the water helps reduce the cooking time.

Yellow Plum and Lavender Chutney

Makes 7 half-pints

Prep time: 20 minutes
Cook time: 35 to 55 minutes

Processing time: 10 minutes
Curing time: 24 hours

CAN THIS   **BUMPER CROP**

This is a variation on one of my first homemade chutneys, and I can't believe it took me so long to try these sweet-tangy condiments. I was stuck in a mindset that these fruit-based sauces were only appropriate with Indian-spiced vegetables, but I've since learned to love them in many fusion pairings. This golden chutney is delicious with many strong flavors, like stinky cheese and wild salmon.

4½ pounds golden plums, chopped (10 cups)

2 medium onions, finely chopped (1 cup)

Zest and juice of 1 lemon (or 3 tablespoons bottled lemon juice [5% acidity])

3 tablespoons peeled, minced fresh ginger

1¾ cups brown sugar

¾ cup white wine vinegar (5% acidity)

1½ tablespoons yellow mustard seeds

1½ teaspoons Morton pickling salt

¼ teaspoon red pepper flakes

2½ tablespoons fresh lavender flowers or 2½ teaspoons dried lavender flowers

¼ cup bottled lemon juice (5% acidity)

1. In a wide 8-quart or larger pot, place the plums, onions, lemon zest (if using), lemon juice, and ginger. Stir in the sugar, vinegar, mustard seeds, salt, and red pepper flakes. Bring to a boil over medium heat, stirring often. Lower the heat to medium-low and boil gently, stirring occasionally, for 25 to 35 minutes, until the chutney starts to thicken.

2. Tie the lavender into a cheesecloth bag and add the bag to the thickened chutney. Continue to boil gently and stir frequently for an additional 10 to 20 minutes, until the chutney is thick enough to cling to a spoon. Remove from the heat, remove the spice bag, and stir in the ¼ cup of bottled lemon juice.

3. Ladle the hot chutney into seven clean, hot ½-pint jars; leave ½ inch of headspace. Remove any air bubbles with a bamboo or wooden chopstick and wipe each jar's rim. Cap the jars with two-piece canning lids.

4. Process in a boiling-water bath for 10 minutes, plus your altitude adjustment (see page 191). Store the jars in a dry, dark, cool place for at least 24 hours before eating. The chutney is best eaten within a year.

Ingredient Tip: If you have a zester, use that to zest the lemon; otherwise, you may want to finely chop the zest so that it blends into the chutney. If you aren't growing lavender at home, check at your local farmers' market, where fresh lavender may be available in summer months. Grocers and specialty stores with a wide stock of bulk herbs and spices often carry dried lavender. If you don't spot it, look among the tea ingredients. You could put the lavender in the jars, but the flavor grows quite strong after a few months.

Quick Tomatillo Salsa

Makes 2 cups   **Prep time:** 10 minutes   **Curing time:** 15 minutes

Traditional green salsas have a tomatillo base. If you haven't yet fallen for these small fruits enclosed in a Chinese lantern–shaped husk like a gift-wrapped treat, start with this recipe. You just need a handful of tomatillos, which are increasingly available in produce sections. Once you're hooked, try growing your own. You'll need a pair of plants to cross-pollinate, but otherwise treat them much like tomatoes. They can be prolific in a warm climate or greenhouse.

6 tomatillos, chopped (1¼ cups)

½ small red onion, finely chopped (¼ cup)

2 garlic cloves, minced

1 Anaheim chile, finely chopped (⅓ cup)

½ Fresno chile, minced (1½ tablespoons)

4 tablespoons finely chopped fresh cilantro

Zest and juice of 1 lime, or 2 tablespoons bottled lime juice (5% acidity)

¼ teaspoon Diamond Crystal kosher salt or ⅛ teaspoon sea salt

1. In a medium bowl, toss together the tomatillos, onion, garlic, and both chiles. Add the cilantro and toss until the vegetables are coated.

2. In a small measuring cup, whisk together the lime zest and juice (or the 2 tablespoons bottled juice) and salt, stirring until the salt dissolves. Stir the brine into the vegetables until coated.

3. Let sit for about 15 minutes, then taste and adjust the seasonings as needed before serving. This salsa will keep for several days in a clean lidded container in the refrigerator.

Try It With: Serve this salsa over firm grilled fish, like halibut or swordfish, or dolloped on omelets or crab cakes. Drain excess liquid and use it as a garnish for guacamole or another dip, or simply dip tortilla chips or pita bread straight into it.

Corn, Bell Pepper, and Black Bean Salsa

Makes 2½ cups   **Prep time:** 10 minutes   **Curing time:** 15 minutes

This quick salsa pairs summer vegetables with black beans and a tangy blend of rice vinegar and lime juice. Savor these raw, fresh flavors straight from the garden, or, for another variation, you can grill or roast the corn, pepper, onion, and garlic (doubling down on the garlic) before tossing the ingredients together. Don't hesitate to double this recipe; the bowl empties quickly.

1½ cups corn kernels (cut from 2 ears)

½ bell pepper, diced (½ cup)

¼ small red onion, finely chopped (2 tablespoons)

2 garlic cloves, minced

2 tablespoons minced fresh cilantro

½ cup canned black beans, rinsed and drained

2 tablespoons unseasoned rice vinegar (4.3% acidity)

Juice of 1 lime, or 2 tablespoons bottled lime juice (5% acidity)

1 teaspoon ground cumin

¼ teaspoon Diamond Crystal kosher salt or ⅛ teaspoon sea salt

1. In a medium bowl, mix the corn, bell pepper, onion, garlic, cilantro, and black beans, tossing to combine.

2. In a small measuring cup, whisk together the vinegar, lime juice, cumin, and salt. Stir the brine into the vegetables until coated.

3. Let sit for about 15 minutes, then taste and adjust the seasonings as needed before serving. This salsa will keep for up to 1 week in a clean lidded container in the refrigerator.

Ingredient Tip: If you're cooking dry black beans for another dish, throw some extra in the pot for this salsa. If you're using commercially canned beans, look for the brand with no additional flavorings and the least amount of salt.

Green Tomato Salsa

Makes 2½ cups   **Prep time:** 10 minutes   **Curing time:** 15 minutes

CAN THIS

I grow tomatillos, so I typically turn to them for salsa verde and margarita mix, reserving my midsummer green tomatoes for fried or pickled curried slices (see Curried Green Tomatoes, page 79). You can substitute this recipe when you want a green sauce. Use it atop firm grilled fish, spread it into cheese quesadillas, or stuff equal parts salsa and black beans in potatoes.

2 large green tomatoes, chopped (1½ cups)

½ red bell pepper, chopped (½ cup)

¼ large sweet onion, finely chopped (6 tablespoons)

1 serrano chile, minced (1 tablespoon)

2 garlic cloves, minced

2 teaspoons minced fresh cilantro

½ teaspoon ground cumin

3 tablespoons red wine vinegar (5% acidity)

Zest and juice of ½ lime, or 1 tablespoon bottled lime juice (5% acidity)

1 teaspoon Diamond Crystal kosher salt

1. In a medium bowl, toss together the tomatoes, bell pepper, onion, chile, and garlic. Add the cilantro and cumin and toss until the vegetables are coated.

2. In a small measuring cup, whisk together the vinegar, lime zest and juice (or 1 tablespoon bottled juice), and salt, stirring until the salt dissolves. Stir the brine into the vegetables until coated.

3. Let sit for about 15 minutes, then taste and adjust the seasonings as needed before serving. This salsa will keep for up to 1 week in a clean lidded container in the refrigerator.

Switch Things Up: For a smoother texture, puree the salsa with an immersion blender or in a food processor. For a thicker one, cook it over medium-low heat for up to 15 minutes. For more heat, add an extra chile. To can this fresh recipe in a boiling-water bath, multiply the ingredients by the number of pint jars you want. Fill and cap the jars as explained in "Canning, Step by Step" (page 6), leaving ½ inch of headspace, and process for 20 minutes, plus your altitude adjustment (see page 191).

Carrot-Top Greens and Mint Salsa

Makes 1¼ cups　　　　**Prep time:** 10 minutes　　　　**Curing time:** 15 minutes to 24 hours

I encourage top-to-root eating, as well as reaching for your homemade condiments while cooking. This quick salsa does both, combining leftover carrot-top greens with other garden tidbits and condiment recipes from this book. The key word is *fresh*, meaning you'll want to go from garden to table as directly as possible. The salsa will lose its bright color the longer it sits but will gain a softer texture and more consistent flavor.

1 cup minced carrot-top greens

½ cup minced fresh mint

½ cup minced fresh flat-leaf parsley

2 scallions or the green top of 1 bulb onion, chopped (¼ cup)

¼ cup capers or Pickled Nasturtium Seeds (page 76), chopped

¼ cup white wine vinegar (5% acidity)

Zest and juice of ½ lemon, or 1½ tablespoons bottled lemon juice (5% acidity)

½ teaspoon Diamond Crystal kosher salt or ¼ teaspoon sea salt

½ teaspoon prepared sriracha or Scratch-Made Sriracha (page 130)

1. In a small bowl, combine the carrot-top greens, mint, and parsley. Mix in the scallions and capers.

2. In a small measuring cup, whisk together the vinegar, lemon zest (if using), lemon juice, salt, and sriracha, stirring until the salt dissolves. Stir the brine into the carrot-top mixture until coated. Let sit at least 15 minutes before tossing with hot roasted vegetables, if you choose. For cold use, transfer to a clean lidded container and refrigerate for 24 hours before using. Store the jar in the refrigerator for up to 1 week.

Try It With: Toss this all-green salsa with colorful roasted or grilled vegetables. Turn it into a dip for chips or vegetables by adding a couple of pureed tomatoes or ½ cup of plain yogurt. Whisk in olive oil to make a salad dressing or grilled fish marinade.

Quick Pineapple and Apple Salsa

Makes 3 cups   **Prep time:** 10 minutes   **Curing time:** 15 to 30 minutes

Pineapple deserves more credit as a salsa anchor: It soaks up flavors, and its natural sweetness pairs well with tangy, salty, and spicy ingredients. It infuses so well that you can make this salsa with pre-pickled pineapple and just the produce. To get every ounce of flavor from a pineapple, use the peel, top, and core in Tepache (page 188).

¼ medium fresh pineapple (1 pound) or 2 cups Pickled Pineapple (page 167), diced

1 medium apple, diced (1 cup)

1 large shallot, minced (¼ cup)

2 tablespoons finely chopped fresh cilantro

½ teaspoon ground cumin (optional)

¼ teaspoon Morton pickling salt or sea salt (optional)

Zest and juice of ½ lime, or 1 tablespoon bottled lime juice (5% acidity) (optional)

1. In a medium bowl, toss together the pineapple, apple, and shallot. Add the cilantro and toss again. If using, sprinkle with the cumin, salt, and lime zest and juice (to taste if using Pickled Pineapple), then toss until the vegetables are coated.

2. Refrigerate for 15 to 30 minutes, until chilled. Taste and adjust the seasonings as needed before serving cold. This salsa will keep for several days in a clean lidded container in the refrigerator.

Try It With: Whether you use fresh or pickled pineapple, this salsa stays mild enough to serve with spice-rubbed meats, chipotle- or wasabi-marinated fish or shrimp, or curry-dusted vegetables.

Grilled Cherry Tomato and Corn Salsa

Makes 7 pints

Prep time: 20 minutes, plus 20 minutes soaking time
Cook time: 20 to 25 minutes

Processing time: 15 minutes
Curing time: 1 week

CAN THIS   **BUMPER CROP**

Grilled vegetables add a charred flavor that works well in cooked salsas; it's an extra but easy step. But loose cherry tomatoes are hard to manage on a grill grate. If you grow your own, harvest them in bunches with their stems and vines attached or thread pre-picked tomatoes onto bamboo skewers. A grill or drip pan can help retain their juice. Alternatively, you could roast all the vegetables or stick with fresh.

2¼ pounds fresh corn (cut from 7 ears)

4 pounds cherry tomatoes (8 cups)

4 poblano chiles, halved lengthwise (¾ cup grilled and chopped)

1 large red onion, halved crosswise (1 cup grilled and diced)

4 dried chipotle chiles or other smoked chiles, crumbled

2½ cups apple cider vinegar (5% acidity)

1 tablespoon ground cumin

2 teaspoons ground coriander

2 teaspoons Morton pickling salt

½ cup finely chopped fresh cilantro

7 tablespoons bottled lime juice (5% acidity)

1. For each ear of corn, carefully peel back enough husk to remove the silk. Fold the husks back over the corn, then submerge the ears in a bowl or pan of cold water for about 20 minutes; soak the bamboo skewers (if using) as well. Remove the skewers and drain the corn.

2. Thread the tomatoes on the bamboo skewers (if using). Oil a medium-hot grill or preheat a grill or drip pan. Grill the tomatoes for about 3 minutes, turning as needed, until they're charred and starting to blister. Transfer to a large bowl to cool. Place the corn directly on the hot grill. Add the poblano chiles and onion, cut-side down; cover and cook for 6 to 8 minutes, venting the grill and turning the vegetables as needed, until the corn husks and chiles are lightly charred and the onion is somewhat softened. Remove from the grill and let cool.

3. Remove any remaining stems from the tomatoes and quarter them. Add the tomatoes and their juices to a large stockpot. Strip the corn kernels from the cobs and chop the poblano chiles and onion; add these to the stockpot and bring to a boil. Add the chipotle chiles, vinegar, cumin, coriander, and salt. Lower the heat and simmer on low for about 10 minutes, stirring to dissolve the salt, until the salsa starts to thicken. Return to just a boil, then remove from the heat and stir in the cilantro.

4. Add 1 tablespoon of lime juice to each of seven clean, hot pint jars, then ladle in the hot salsa; leave ½ inch of headspace. Wipe the rims and cap the jars with two-piece canning lids. Add the jars to a boiling-water bath.

5. Process the salsa in the boiling-water bath for 15 minutes, plus your altitude adjustment (see page 191). Store the jars in a dry, dark, cool place for at least 1 week before eating. The salsa is best eaten within a year.

Ingredient Tip: Chipotle chiles are also sold canned in adobo, but this sauce overpowers the bright flavor of the cherry tomatoes and corn. Look for whole dried chipotle chiles with other dried chiles or in the spice section of your market.

Chinese-Inspired Plum Sauce

Makes 7 half-pints

Prep time: 25 minutes
Cook time: 1 hour 5 minutes
to 1 hour 15 minutes

Processing time: 10 minutes
Curing time: 24 hours

CAN THIS   **BUMPER CROP**

This plum sauce bears little resemblance to jelly-like sauces squeezed from little packets onto American Chinese takeout. It also varies from more home-style Chinese plum sauce recipes that combine round, juicy plums with another fruit. All of its fruit flavor comes from Italian prune plums, which grow well in my northern, mountainous area. I'd even classify this flavorful sauce as a chutney because of its sweet fruit–tangy vinegar flavor. It's delicious with Asian dishes.

3 pounds Italian prune plums, coarsely chopped (7 cups)

1 large red bell pepper, coarsely chopped (1 cup)

1 small red onion, coarsely chopped (1 cup)

3 garlic cloves, minced

2 red serrano chiles or jalapeño peppers, coarsely chopped (2½ tablespoons)

3 tablespoons peeled, minced fresh ginger

1¼ cups brown sugar

2 cups apple cider vinegar (5% acidity)

⅓ cup sake or dry sherry

2½ teaspoons soy sauce

1 (4-inch) cinnamon stick

1. In a wide 8-quart or larger pot, combine the plums, bell pepper, onion, garlic, chiles, and ginger. Stir in the sugar, vinegar, sake, soy sauce, and cinnamon stick. Bring to a boil over medium heat, stirring often. Lower the heat to medium-low and boil gently, stirring occasionally, for about 1 hour, until the sauce starts to thicken.

2. Remove from the heat and pull out the cinnamon stick. Puree the plum sauce in the pot using an immersion blender, or carefully transfer it to an upright blender or food processor to puree. Return the sauce to the pot and simmer over medium-low heat for 5 to 15 minutes, until hot and thick.

3. Ladle the hot plum sauce into seven clean, hot ½-pint jars; leave ¼ inch of headspace. Remove any air bubbles with a bamboo or wooden chopstick and wipe each jar's rim. Cap the jars with two-piece canning lids.

4. Process in a boiling-water bath for 10 minutes, plus your altitude adjustment (see page 191). Store the jars in a dry, dark, cool place for at least 24 hours before using. The sauce is best eaten within a year.

Try It With: Toss this sauce into stir-fries and noodle dishes for a sweet-and-sour flavor. It's the perfect seasoning for two-ingredient rice meals, like tofu and broccoli or asparagus and shrimp. It also works as a dipping sauce; just thin it with a little water when serving.

Romesco-Style Roasted Pepper Sauce

Makes 1½ cups

Prep time: 20 minutes, plus 5 to 10 minutes cooling time
Cook time: 2 to 4 minutes

Curing time: 2 hours in the brine, plus 30 minutes as the sauce

American palates have become accustomed to a roasted red pepper version of romesco, traditionally made with tomatoes and a mix of sweet and hot peppers. This version takes it a step further, roasting the peppers and then pickling them slightly before creating the sauce. The brine brings out the peppers' flavor, far beyond what you'll taste in a store-bought jar of marinated peppers.

3 medium red bell peppers (1¼ pounds)

2 garlic cloves, peeled

2 tablespoons white wine vinegar (5% acidity)

Juice of ⅓ lemon or 1 tablespoon bottled lemon juice (5% acidity)

1 tablespoon olive oil, or more to adjust thickness

¼ cup roasted almonds

2 tablespoons fresh oregano or 2 teaspoons dried oregano

1 teaspoon sugar

1 teaspoon Morton pickling salt or sea salt

1 ancho chile or other dried smoked chile

1. Preheat the broiler to high, with a rack placed high in the oven.

2. Put the whole peppers on a baking sheet and broil for 2 to 4 minutes, turning frequently, until most of the skin is charred and blistered. Enclose them in a brown paper bag or damp cloth for 5 to 10 minutes, until cool enough to handle, and peel off the skin and remove the stems, cores, and seeds.

3. In a medium bowl, combine the roasted peppers and garlic. Add the vinegar, lemon juice, and 1 tablespoon of olive oil. Toss to combine, then cover with a dish towel and let sit for at least 2 hours.

4. In a food processor, coarsely grind the almonds; add the oregano, sugar, salt, and chile, then process until finely ground. Add the roasted peppers, garlic, and brine, then process until smooth. Thin to your desired thickness with additional olive oil and taste and adjust the seasonings as needed.

5. Let sit for 30 minutes at room temperature before serving. For longer storage, transfer the sauce to a clean lidded container and refrigerate for up to 1 week; bring the sauce back to room temperature and stir before serving.

Switch Things Up: Amid summer's heat, throw fresh peppers on the grill to avoid raising your house temperature. Almonds are traditional in Spanish romesco, but you can substitute hazelnuts or other nuts.

Chermoula (North African–Inspired Herb Sauce)

Makes 1 (4-ounce) jar   **Prep time:** 10 minutes   **Curing time:** 24 hours

Chermoula comes from North Africa, where it's often served with fish and shellfish. You'll find it referred to as a sauce, relish, and marinade; it can be used in all those ways, but the finished texture most closely resembles pesto. Its intense herb-and-spice tones enhance tagines and other long-cooked dishes. Use it to marinate shrimp, meat, and vegetables before skewering and grilling them as kebabs.

4 garlic cloves, peeled

1 (1-inch) piece peeled fresh ginger

¼ cup chopped fresh flat-leaf parsley

⅓ cup chopped fresh cilantro

Zest and juice of 1 large lemon or ¼ cup bottled lemon juice (5% acidity)

2 teaspoons sweet paprika

Pinch cayenne powder

2 teaspoons ground cumin

¼ teaspoon Morton pickling salt or sea salt

¼ cup olive oil

1. In a food processor, grind the garlic and ginger to a paste. Add the parsley, cilantro, and lemon zest (if using) and process until finely chopped. Add the lemon juice, paprika, cayenne, cumin, and salt and puree until smooth.

2. Pour the puree into a medium measuring cup. Pour in the olive oil slowly, mixing with a fork or whisk so that the sauce emulsifies. Taste and adjust the seasonings as needed.

3. For the best flavor, pack the chermoula into a clean 4-ounce jar, screw on a nonreactive lid, and refrigerate for at least 24 hours. Before serving, bring it to room temperature and whisk again until emulsified. This sauce will keep for up to 2 weeks in the refrigerator.

Ingredient Tip: If you don't have a food processor, cut everything as finely as possible. A ginger grater or mortar and pestle will work best for making the garlic-and-ginger paste. If the sauce remains too thick after it's returned to room temperature, add lemon juice to taste and olive oil.

Harissa (North African–Inspired Chile Paste)

Makes 1 (4-ounce) jar

Prep time: 10 minutes, plus 30 minutes to 1 hour soaking time

Tunisia claims ownership of this classic condiment made with dried chiles, but variations have spread across North Africa and the Middle East. This version resembles one I enjoyed in Morocco but is made with dried chiles that are readily available in the United States. Guajillo chiles are dried mirasol chiles; they're somewhat sweet but have a bit of heat, like mild fresh jalapeños. Anchos, or dried poblanos, are less spicy with smoky overtones.

6 or 7 guajillo chiles or
2 or 3 ancho chiles
(1½ ounces)

9 garlic cloves

1½ teaspoons Morton pickling salt

2 teaspoons ground cumin

2 teaspoons ground coriander

Juice of 1 lemon or
3 tablespoons bottled lemon juice (5% acidity)

2 tablespoons olive oil

1. Remove the stems and, if desired, the seeds from the dried chiles. Soak them in hot water for 30 minutes to 1 hour, until soft, then drain.

2. Using a food processor, finely chop the rehydrated chiles and garlic. Add the salt, cumin, coriander, and lemon juice and puree until smooth. Pour the puree into a medium measuring cup. Slowly pour in up to 1 tablespoon of olive oil, mixing with a fork or whisk so that the paste emulsifies. Taste and adjust the seasonings as needed.

3. Use the harissa immediately, or pack it into a clean ½-pint jar, topping with enough of the remaining olive oil to cover the surface of the puree. Screw on a nonreactive lid and store in the refrigerator for up to 3 months.

Don't Forget: Peppers that are later dried often aged longer on the plant, building up capsaicin, which releases readily when they're rehydrated, so it's best to wear rubber gloves when handling them. Guajillos and anchos can be combined or replaced by other chiles for milder or hotter paste.

Try It With: Harissa traditionally accompanies or is stirred into couscous dishes and stews. You can toss it with vegetables before roasting or shrimp before grilling. A couple of tablespoons are delicious coating mixed olives or baked chickpeas for a snack.

Ajvar (Roasted Pepper and Eggplant Sauce)

Makes 2 half-pints

Prep time: 10 minutes
Cook time: 1 hour 10 minutes
to 1 hour 40 minutes

Curing time: 2 days

In an eggplant bumper crop year, I stumbled onto a version of this Serbian sauce, and I've enjoyed it enough to add an extra plant to my greenhouse and grill up batches throughout the summer. You can oven-roast or grill the vegetables instead of pan-roasting them, but don't skimp on the puree's stove-top time; the goal is to reduce the mixture to the thickness of tomato paste before the vinegar thins it to a sauce.

1 tablespoon olive oil

2 long (12 ounces) Italian or Japanese eggplants, peeled and cut into ¾-inch-thick slices

3 medium red bell peppers (1¼ pounds), each cut lengthwise into 6 strips

2 garlic cloves, peeled and thinly sliced

1½ teaspoons Morton pickling salt

1 tablespoon sugar

¼ cup plus 2 tablespoons apple cider vinegar (5% acidity)

1. In a large skillet, heat the olive oil over medium heat and cook the eggplant slices for about 5 minutes, until lightly browned; flip the slices, add the bell peppers and garlic, and cook for another 5 minutes, until the peppers are blistered and the eggplant and garlic are browned. Transfer to a plate lined with paper towels to cool and drain, patting away any excess oil.

2. In a food processor, pulse the peppers, eggplant, and garlic to puree. Add the salt and sugar. Pulse a few times to combine into a coarse paste, or puree until smooth.

3. Transfer the puree to a clean large skillet and cook over medium-low heat for about 1 hour, stirring occasionally, until the puree thickens and looks like tomato paste; if it's still thin, continue cooking for another 30 minutes or so, stirring frequently to keep the paste from sticking to the pan. Stir in the vinegar and bring the mixture to a boil.

4. Pack the paste into two clean ½-pint jars, removing any air bubbles with a bamboo or wooden chopstick. Screw on nonreactive lids and refrigerate for 2 days before using. The paste will keep for months in the refrigerator.

Ingredient Tip: You can weigh out 12 ounces of a larger or smaller eggplant variety, such as a globe eggplant or mini container-grown eggplant. I split the sauce into two jars and keep the second sealed until the first is empty.

Try It With: Ajvar thickens enough that you can use it as a dip or spread, but I tend to cook with it, tossing it with pasta or roasted vegetables. It's delicious as a relish for grilled fish, and inland Balkan communities might use it to accompany lamb or other meats.

Don't Forget: If you remove any air bubbles and always dip into the jar with a clean spoon, you'll reduce contamination that could make the paste spoil more quickly.

Vinegar-Based Horseradish Paste

Makes 1 half-pint   **Prep time:** 10 minutes   **Curing time:** 24 hours

Plant one piece of horseradish root, and you'll never run out. This perennial digs deep and spreads readily, so put it in a permanent location away from your other beds. You can then make your own prepared horseradish quickly and in a small amount. It's a vast improvement on commercial brands because your jar won't need preservatives but will still retain its sharp bite to the last spoonful.

4 ounces peeled horseradish root, grated (⅔ cup)

⅓ cup white wine vinegar (5% or higher acidity)

⅓ teaspoon Morton pickling salt

1. Use a food processor with a shredder attachment to grate the horseradish. Switch to a chopping blade, stir in the vinegar and salt, and process the root until a smooth paste forms.

2. Pack the paste into a clean ½-pint jar. Screw on a nonreactive lid and refrigerate for at least 24 hours before using. Prepared horseradish will keep for several months but will start to lose its potency after a few weeks.

Don't Forget: Keep your face away from the horseradish as you work: Fresh horseradish is even more of a tearjerker than old onions. If you don't have a food processor, you can grate the root using a large-holed cheese grater and puree the paste with an immersion blender.

German-Inspired Spicy Mustard

Makes 1 (12-ounce) jar

Prep time: 25 minutes, plus 3 or more hours soaking and 30 minutes cooling time

Curing time: 4 days

If you've never made mustard, you'll be surprised by how delicious and easy it can be. This recipe creates my go-to scratch-made mustard. It's vegan, gluten-free, and speckled with whole seeds, although you could grind it completely smooth. Don't be daunted by the long ingredient list. The layers of flavor come through in the finished blend, but you can alter or leave out the last few spices if you don't have them on hand.

¼ cup yellow mustard seeds

2 tablespoons brown mustard seeds

¼ cup powdered mustard

½ cup cold water

1 cup apple cider vinegar (5% acidity)

1 small onion, finely chopped (¼ cup)

2 garlic cloves, minced

2 tablespoons brown sugar

1 teaspoon Morton pickling salt

¾ teaspoon fresh tarragon or ¼ teaspoon dried tarragon

½ teaspoon ground cinnamon

¼ teaspoon dill seeds

¼ teaspoon ground allspice

⅛ teaspoon ground turmeric

1. In a large measuring cup, combine the yellow and brown mustard seeds. Add the powdered mustard then the water, stirring until thoroughly blended. Let the seeds soak at room temperature for at least 3 hours.

2. In a small saucepan, bring the vinegar, onion, garlic, sugar, salt, tarragon, cinnamon, dill seeds, allspice, and turmeric to a simmer over medium heat and cook, uncovered, for 10 to 15 minutes, until reduced by at least half. Let the brine infuse for about 30 minutes, until it has cooled to room temperature.

3. Strain the vinegar mixture through a fine-mesh colander into the mustard mixture and puree with an immersion blender to your desired texture. Alternatively, transfer both the strained liquid and the mustard mixture to a food processor and pulse to combine.

4. Scrape the mustard into a clean 12-ounce jar, cover loosely with a nonreactive lid, and let sit at room temperature for 24 hours. Screw down the lid and refrigerate for at least 3 days before using. It will keep for at least a year in the refrigerator.

Switch Things Up: Yellow seeds are milder than brown ones, so change their ratio for a more or less pungent spread. You can swap in beer, wine, brandy, or apple cider for some or all of the water. The sugar can also be adjusted to taste or replaced by honey.

Swedish-Inspired Hot Mustard

Makes 1 (12-ounce) jar **Prep time:** 15 minutes, plus 30 minutes cooling time **Cook time:** 10 minutes **Curing time:** 2 days

I remember my uncle making this traditional, spicy mustard in my childhood, long before my taste buds could handle its heat. The bite of straight dry mustard blasts through the sweet layers of sugar, honey, and cider. My uncle's original recipe made a double batch; don't hesitate to do the same, especially if you want to divide it into 4- or 8-ounce jars for gifting.

2 eggs, beaten

¼ cup brown sugar

¼ cup honey

¼ cup apple cider

¼ cup apple cider vinegar (5% acidity)

¼ cup powdered mustard

1½ teaspoons all-purpose flour

¼ teaspoon ground cardamom

¼ teaspoon ground cloves

1. In a small saucepan, combine the beaten eggs, sugar, and honey, stirring until thoroughly blended. Mix in the cider, vinegar, powdered mustard, flour, cardamom, and cloves. Cook the mixture over low heat, stirring constantly, for about 10 minutes, until it thickens. Let sit for about 30 minutes, until it has cooled to room temperature.

2. Scrape the mustard into a clean 12-ounce jar. Screw on a nonreactive lid and refrigerate for at least 2 days before using. It will keep for at least 6 months in the refrigerator.

Don't Forget: Because of the eggs and flour, this mustard needs to be cooked slightly and should mellow in the refrigerator before you use it, rather than sitting at room temperature.

Try It With: My uncle liked to serve this mustard with a variety of sausages and cured meats, as well as with a salty Smithfield ham at Christmas. I spread it on homemade sourdough bagels with smoked salmon and goat cheese or toss it with roasted potatoes.

Sweet-and-Tart Blueberries, page 159

Sweet and Fruity Pickles

Miso-Brined Apples

Makes 1 pint

Prep time: 10 minutes, plus 1 hour salting time

Curing time: 2 to 24 hours

The same type of miso pickling bed used for vegetables works well for firm fruit, such as apples and pears. Although pre-salting to pull moisture from the produce improves miso pickles' texture and flavor and makes the pickling bed last longer, fresh fruit has so much natural juice that it's best eaten within a couple of days. I pickle one apple at a time so that it doesn't sit too long and become overly soft.

1 large Granny Smith or other tart, firm apple

1 teaspoon Diamond Crystal kosher salt

½ cup white miso

1 tablespoon sake

½ teaspoon sugar

1. Peel, halve, and core the apple before cutting it into ¼-inch-thick slices. Place the slices in a colander set over a bowl, toss with the salt, and let the excess moisture drain for 1 hour. Rinse, drain again, and pat dry with a dish towel.

2. In a small measuring cup, mix together the miso, sake, and sugar.

3. At the bottom of a clean, wide-mouth pint jar, spread a thin layer of the miso mixture and top with a layer of apple; continue alternating the layers until all the slices are coated and fill the jar. Spread the remaining miso mixture over the top, completely covering the uppermost slices. Cover the jar with a nonreactive lid and refrigerate for 2 to 24 hours.

4. To serve, remove the apple slices from the pickling bed, wiping excess miso back into the jar with your fingers. If they seem too salty, rinse off the remaining miso under cool running water and pat the slices dry. The apples are best eaten in 3 days but will keep for about a week in the refrigerator.

Try It With: Eat these apples on toast spread with peanut butter or goat cheese, in tuna salad, or with other fresh and pickled vegetables in a rice bowl. The pickling bed can be reused for additional apples; once the juice saturates it, use the miso as a shrimp marinade.

Jerk-Spiced Banana Pickles

Makes 1 pint

Prep time: 20 minutes, plus 30 minutes cooling time

Cook time: 11 minutes, plus 5 minutes infusing time
Curing time: 1 hour

Bananas often get a sugary treatment, especially when fully ripe. But the green ones add mild sweetness to spicy, sour brine. This blend uses the dominant flavors of Jamaican jerk seasoning: allspice, Scotch bonnet chile, thyme, and ginger.

1¼ cups white wine vinegar (5% acidity)

5 tablespoons turbinado or brown sugar

1 teaspoon Morton pickling salt

4 slices peeled, fresh ginger

½ Scotch bonnet chile, seeded

Zest and juice of ½ lime

4 black peppercorns

2 allspice berries

1 teaspoon fresh thyme or ½ teaspoon dried thyme

2 or 3 green bananas, peeled and cut into ¼-inch-thick diagonal slices (1½ cups)

1. In a medium saucepan, bring the vinegar, sugar, and salt to a boil, stirring to dissolve the sugar and salt. Add the ginger, chile, lime zest and juice, peppercorns, allspice, and thyme, then lower the heat to medium-low and simmer, covered, for 10 minutes, until slightly thickened. Add the bananas, cook for 1 minute, then remove the pan from the heat and let it sit, covered, for 5 minutes, just until the bananas can be pricked with a fork.

2. Use a slotted spoon to transfer the hot banana slices and ginger into a clean wide-mouth pint jar, packing them gently up to the shoulder of the jar. Let the brine sit for about 30 minutes, until it has cooled to room temperature. Remove the chile.

3. Ladle the brine over the bananas so that they are submerged but the brine is about ½ inch from the jar's rim. Screw on a nonreactive lid and refrigerate for at least 1 hour before eating. They will keep for weeks in the refrigerator.

Switch Things Up: Traditional Scotch bonnet chiles pack intense heat, clocking in at 100,000 to 350,000 Scoville heat units. For less heat, swap in a Fresno chile (2,500 to 10,000 SHU) or 1 teaspoon of leftover mash from Scratch-Made Sriracha (page 130).

Try It With: The pickle pairs well with jerk-marinated chicken or pork or pan-fried tofu and mixed vegetables over rice.

Sweet-Spiced Blackberries

Makes 1 (12-ounce) jar

Prep time: 10 minutes, plus 30 minutes cooling time

Curing time: 2 to 8 hours

Delicate berries are best preserved in the freezer or as jam. But when you tire of the standard overly sweet preparations, a quick pickle can renew your interest in blackberries' juicy pop. Blackberries soften quickly in the brine, so I make this pickle in small batches even when I have a large harvest; double or triple the recipe for a family gathering.

⅓ cup white wine vinegar (5% acidity)

⅓ cup water

1 teaspoon honey

½ teaspoon Morton pickling salt

½ teaspoon Sweet-Savory Spice Blend (page 16)

¼ teaspoon fresh thyme or ⅛ teaspoon dried thyme

1 strip lemon peel

1 small bay leaf

¾ cup (6 ounces) fresh blackberries

1. In a medium saucepan, bring the vinegar, water, honey, and salt to a boil, stirring to dissolve the honey and salt. Remove the pan from the heat and add the spice blend, thyme, lemon peel, and bay leaf; let the brine infuse for about 30 minutes, until it has cooled to room temperature.

2. Strain the brine through a colander into a large measuring cup.

3. Gently transfer the colander's contents to the bottom of a clean 12-ounce jar. Add the berries. Pour the brine over the berries so that they are submerged but the brine is about ½ inch from the jar's rim. Screw on a nonreactive lid and refrigerate for 2 to 8 hours before eating. Leftover pickles can be stored in the refrigerator but are best eaten within 3 days.

Try It With: The drained berries can be displayed on a pickle tray with mild cheeses, paired with shortbread cookies, or dropped into cocktails. Set them atop ricotta-spread baguette slices for crostini, or serve them alongside grilled fish or meat.

Sweet-and-Tart Blueberries

Makes 1 quart

Prep time: 10 minutes, plus 30 minutes cooling time

Curing time: 3 days

I think of blueberries as a delicate fruit, but every time I infuse them I'm surprised by how long they take to absorb additional flavors. So although you can eat these berries in just a few hours, letting them sit several days brings the vinegar and lavender flavors into the berries. They'll start to soften after about a week but will continue to pick up flavor beyond that.

¾ cup apple cider vinegar (5% acidity)

¾ cup water

3 tablespoons sugar

1 tablespoon Morton pickling salt

4 lavender sprigs (3 tablespoons flowers) or 1 tablespoon dried lavender blossoms

2⅔ cups blueberries (1 pound)

1. In a small saucepan, bring the vinegar, water, sugar, and salt to a boil, stirring to dissolve the sugar and salt. Remove the pan from the heat and add the lavender; let the brine infuse for about 30 minutes, until it has cooled to room temperature.

2. Gently put the blueberries into a clean wide-mouth quart jar, removing the lavender sprigs from the brine and sliding them down the jar's side as you fill it. Ladle the brine over the berries so that they are submerged but the brine is about ½ inch from the jar's rim. Screw on a nonreactive lid and refrigerate for at least 3 days before eating. They will keep for a couple of weeks in the refrigerator.

Ingredient Tip: If the lavender flavor becomes too strong for your taste buds, simply pull out the sprigs, or strain the brine to remove separated blossoms, and return the jar to the refrigerator.

Try It With: I like these pickles with goat cheese and sourdough pita bread or grilled salmon and on salad and pizza. Once you've eaten all the berries, use the brine in a mocktail with orange juice and seltzer water or a cocktail with vodka and lemonade.

Sour Cherry Pickles

Makes 1 pint

Prep time: 20 minutes, plus 30 minutes cooling time

Curing time: 24 hours

Montana's Flathead Valley is known for its sweet cherries; locals and tourists alike call the most popular variety simply "Flathead cherries," even though they're officially Lamberts. But I grew up loving tangy sour, or pie, cherries. They lend themselves well to pickles, although you could swap a sweeter variety into this recipe. I eat pickled cherries straight from the jar, on salads, tossed with peppers and garlic as a quick salsa, or atop ice cream.

⅓ cup apple cider vinegar (5% acidity)

⅓ cup water

2 tablespoons brown sugar

¼ teaspoon Morton pickling salt

1 teaspoon black peppercorns

2 rosemary sprigs (2 tablespoons leaves), divided

¾ pound whole sour cherries, pitted (2⅓ cups)

1. In a small saucepan, bring the vinegar, water, sugar, and salt to a simmer, stirring to dissolve the salt and sugar. Remove the pan from the heat and add the peppercorns and 1 rosemary sprig.

2. Set a fine-mesh colander over the pan, pit the cherries, add the fruit to the colander, and let the juice drain into the brine (see Tip). Once it stops dripping, stir to combine and set the cherries aside. Let the mixture infuse for about 30 minutes, until it has cooled to room temperature.

3. In a clean wide-mouth jar, pack the cherries, adding the remaining rosemary sprig down one side. Remove the spent rosemary sprig from the brine, then ladle the brine over the cherries so that they are submerged but the brine is about ½ inch from the jar's rim. Screw on a non-reactive lid and refrigerate for at least 24 hours before eating. They will keep for weeks in the refrigerator.

Ingredient Tip: Draining the juice into the brine captures the maximum cherry flavor, but it can thicken the brine and might shorten the pickle's storage life, particularly if you substitute sweet cherries. For a clearer brine, strain the juice into a separate cup and put it to another use.

Sweet Pickled Grapes

Makes 1 quart   **Prep time:** 10 minutes, plus 30 minutes cooling time   **Curing time:** 2 days

Grapes require a balancing act as a pickle; after all, they're the key component of many vinegars, with a natural acidity to match. Brined grapes, a classic Persian fermented pickle, rely on naturally sour varieties picked at the peak of their pucker power. But unless you have your own vines, these grapes are rarely available in Western cultures. The more common sweet grapes fare better in vinegar. I choose red over green because the brown sugar darkens the brine a bit, but both will work.

⅔ cup apple cider vinegar (5% acidity)

⅔ cup water

5 tablespoons brown sugar

2 teaspoons Morton pickling salt

2 (2-inch) strips orange peel

4 cups sweet seedless grapes (red or green) (1¼ pounds)

1. In a medium saucepan, bring the vinegar, water, sugar, and salt to a boil, stirring to dissolve the sugar and salt. Remove the pan from the heat and add the orange peel; let the brine infuse for about 30 minutes, until it has cooled to room temperature.

2. Remove the orange peel and place it in the bottom of a clean wide-mouth quart jar. Fill the jar with grapes, packing them firmly but without bruising, up to the shoulder of the jar. Ladle the brine over the fruit so that it is submerged but the brine is about ½ inch from the jar's rim. Screw on a nonreactive lid and refrigerate for at least 2 days before eating. They will keep for a few weeks in the refrigerator.

Pickled Orange Segments

Makes 1 quart

Prep time: 20 minutes, plus 5 to 24 hours macerating and 30 minutes cooling time

Curing time: 24 hours

BUMPER CROP

My first attempts at pickled oranges involved piles of sugar and cooking the fruit until it was closer to marmalade, but with the bitter flavor of the white pith. So I started applying a mixology technique for putting citrus flavor and aroma in cocktails. Letting the orange peels sit in sugar until it sucks up the citrus oil keeps that bright fresh flavor without needing the peels and pith in the jar. I like navel oranges for this recipe because they're easy to zest and the pith comes off well.

3 large oranges (2¼ pounds)

¾ cup sugar

¾ cup white wine vinegar (5% acidity)

¾ teaspoon Morton pickling salt

1 teaspoon black peppercorns

1 (4-inch) cinnamon stick

8 whole cloves

6 slices peeled fresh ginger (optional)

Juice of 2 medium lemons or 6 tablespoons bottled lemon juice (5% acidity)

1. Peel the oranges using a vegetable peeler, trying not to remove the white pith; refrigerate the peeled fruit until ready to use. Place the peels in a clean wide-mouth pint jar, then add the sugar, tossing until the peels are coated. Using a kraut pounder or wooden spoon, press on the mixture until the peels begin to release their oils. Screw on a nonreactive lid and shake. Let sit for at least 5 hours and up to 24 hours, shaking occasionally.

2. Cut a thin slice from the end of each peeled orange, just enough to see the sections. Use a sharp knife to cut a slit down the thickest piece of interior membrane and then pull the orange in half. Peel off the pith, scraping away excess that clings to the orange and keeping the membranes intact as much as possible. Gently pull the orange apart into segments.

3. Using a rubber spatula, scrape the sugared peels into a small saucepan. Add the vinegar, salt, peppercorns, cinnamon, cloves, and ginger and bring just to a simmer, stirring to dissolve the sugar and salt. Remove the pan from the heat and add the orange wedges; cover and let the pickles sit for about 30 minutes, until the brine has cooled to room temperature.

4. Use a slotted spoon to transfer the orange wedges and other flavorings, discarding the orange peels, into a clean wide-mouth quart jar, packing them gently up to the shoulder of the jar. Stir the lemon juice into the brine, then ladle it over the orange wedges so that they are submerged but the brine is about ½ inch from the jar's rim. Screw on a nonreactive lid and refrigerate for at least 24 hours before eating. They will keep for weeks in the refrigerator.

Try it With: Step 1, creating oleo-saccharum, makes an orange-flavored paste or syrup, if dissolved in a little hot water, that will keep for several weeks and can be used in cocktails or other beverages. Try it in an old-fashioned, with pickled orange segments for snacking.

Pickled Mango

Makes 2 pints

Prep time: 20 minutes, plus 30 minutes cooling time

Curing time: 24 hours

In tropical mango-growing countries, hard, green mangos can command a higher price than soft, ripe ones and are snatched up for pickles and other sour condiments. These countries also offer hundreds of mango varieties beyond the ubiquitous but bland Tommy Atkins mangos available throughout the United States. Regardless of variety, choose the firmest fruit available. Unripe mangos soften slightly but hold their shape. For the most flavor, toast the spices (as described in Essential Spice Blends, page 16).

2 medium unripe mangos (1½ pounds)

Zest and juice of ½ lemon or 4 teaspoons bottled lemon juice (5% acidity)

1 teaspoon ground turmeric

¾ cup apple cider vinegar (5% acidity)

¾ cup water

¼ cup sugar

1½ teaspoons Morton pickling salt

1½ teaspoons brown mustard seeds

1 teaspoon cardamom pods

½ teaspoon cumin seeds

4 dried chiles de árbol or other hot chiles, crushed

1. For each mango, cut a thin slice off each end, then peel it with a vegetable peeler. Cut a thick cheek from each side of the pit and remove as much flesh as possible from the pit, then slice the flesh into thin strips. In a medium bowl toss the flesh with the lemon zest (if using) and juice and the turmeric.

2. In a small saucepan, bring the vinegar, water, sugar, and salt to a boil, stirring until the sugar and salt dissolve.

3. Divide the mustard seeds, cardamom, cumin seeds, and chiles between two clean wide-mouth pint jars. Divide the mango strips between the jars.

4. Ladle the hot brine over the mangos so that they are submerged but the brine is about ½ inch from each jar's rim. Cover loosely with a nonreactive lid and let sit until completely cooled, about 30 minutes. Tighten the lid and store in the refrigerator for at least 24 hours, returning to room temperature before eating. They will keep for up to 1 month in the refrigerator.

Try It With: Pickled mangos can accompany almost any meal or stand solo as a snack. Try them alongside grilled meat, atop curried vegetables and rice, or on a salad. Layer them on flatbread with arugula and blue cheese, or stuff them inside pita bread with falafel and tahini sauce.

Quick-Pickled Peaches

Makes 1 pint　　　**Prep time:** 15 minutes, plus 30 minutes cooling time　　　**Curing time:** 4 hours

Pickled peaches make a tangy replacement for the typically overly sweet canned peaches. Blanching makes it easy to remove the skin from just-ripe peaches; avoid hard ones, which will have little flavor and pits that are nearly impossible to remove. Serve these peaches with sourdough waffles at breakfast, on a green salad at lunch or dinner, or over ice cream for dessert.

2 peaches, halved and pitted

¾ cup rice wine vinegar (4.3% acidity)

¼ cup sugar

¼ teaspoon Diamond Crystal kosher salt

1 (2-inch) cinnamon stick

6 slices peeled fresh ginger

1. Bring a large saucepan of water to a boil. Add the peaches, letting them blanch for 30 seconds, then immediately plunge them in a bowl of cold water. When cool, remove the peaches from the water and slip off their skins. Cut the flesh into 1-inch-thick slices.

2. In a medium saucepan, bring the vinegar, sugar, and salt to a boil, stirring to dissolve the sugar and salt. Remove the pan from the heat and add the cinnamon stick and ginger; let the brine infuse for about 30 minutes, until it has cooled to room temperature.

3. Strain the brine through a colander into a large measuring cup.

4. In the bottom of a clean wide-mouth pint jar, place the drained cinnamon stick and ginger. Gently add the peach slices. Ladle the brine over the peaches so that they are submerged but the brine is about ½ inch from the jar's rim. Screw on a nonreactive lid and refrigerate for at least 4 hours before eating. They will keep for a couple of weeks in the refrigerator.

Fresh Pears with Lemon

Makes 1 quart

Prep time: 25 minutes, plus 30 minutes cooling time

Cook time: 1 minute, plus 5 minutes infusing time
Curing time: 3 days

BUMPER CROP

Pear varieties are gaining space in produce sections. In season, you might find crisp Bosc, Asian, and other pears beside the standard soft Bartletts and somewhat firmer D'Anjous. The natural pH of these varieties can range from assuredly acidic to questionable, with many types of Asian pears classified as low acid. Although pickling evens the field, firm pears make the best pickles.

6 medium (2 pounds) firm pears, peeled, quartered, and cored

1 small lemon

1 cup white wine vinegar (5% acidity)

1 cup sugar

¾ teaspoon Morton pickling salt

6 slices peeled fresh ginger

1. In a medium bowl, put the pear pieces. Using a vegetable peeler, cut and add 4 wide strips of lemon zest, then cut the lemon in half and squeeze its juice over the pears; toss to coat.

2. In a medium saucepan, bring the vinegar, sugar, salt, and ginger to a boil, stirring to dissolve the sugar and salt. Lower the heat to medium-low, then add the pears and lemon zest. Cook for 1 minute, then remove the pan from the heat and let it sit, covered, for 5 minutes, just until the pears can be pricked with a fork.

3. Use tongs or a slotted spoon to transfer the hot pears, ginger, and lemon zest into a clean wide-mouth quart jar, packing them gently up to the shoulder of the jar. Let the brine sit for about 30 minutes, until it has cooled to room temperature.

4. Ladle the brine over the pears so that they are submerged but the brine is about ½ inch from the jar's rim. Screw on a nonreactive lid and refrigerate for at least 3 days before eating. They will keep for weeks in the refrigerator.

Ingredient Tip: Use small pears or cut large ones into 6 or 8 wedges. Tiny pears, like Seckels, are easier to pickle with the skin on, but some people dislike the texture. After you finish the pears, use the brine like a shrub (see Strawberry-Balsamic Shrub, page 185).

Pickled Pineapple

Makes 2 pints

Prep time: 20 minutes, plus 30 minutes cooling time

Cook time: 5 minutes
Curing time: 2 days

Pineapple pickles give the fruit a new twist for those living in pineapple-rich areas and boost the flavor of imported pineapples. It's worth buying whole pineapples for pickling; precut pieces will already have released some of their juice and will soften quickly. Don't toss the skin and core; instead, rinse the pineapple under cool running water before cutting it and set the trimmings aside for Tepache (page 188).

1 medium (3½-pound) pineapple or 1¾ pounds fresh pineapple flesh (3¾ cups of 4-inch-long spears)

½ cup red wine vinegar (5% acidity)

½ cup water

¼ cup brown sugar

½ teaspoon Morton pickling salt

1 teaspoon coriander seeds, crushed

½ teaspoon cumin seeds

¼ teaspoon yellow mustard seeds

¼ teaspoon black peppercorns, crushed

1. Twist the leaves off the pineapple, then cut off the top and bottom with a large sharp knife. Stand the pineapple upright and cut off the peel in strips. Remove the remaining eyes with a small knife. Cut the flesh in quarters lengthwise, then cut out the core. Cut the pineapple flesh into 1-inch-thick spears, no more than 4 inches long.

2. In a large saucepan, bring the vinegar, water, sugar, and salt to a boil, stirring to dissolve the sugar and salt. Add the coriander seeds, cumin seeds, mustard seeds, and peppercorns. Lower the heat to low, cover, and simmer for 5 minutes to infuse the flavors. Add the pineapple and return the brine just to a boil. Remove the pan from the heat and let sit for about 30 minutes, until it has cooled to room temperature.

3. Use a slotted spoon to divide the pineapple between two clean wide-mouth pint jars. Ladle the brine over the spears so that they are submerged but the brine is about ½ inch from the jar's rim; evenly divide the spices between the jars. Screw on a nonreactive lid and refrigerate for 2 days before eating. They will keep for more than a month in the refrigerator but are best eaten within a couple of weeks.

Try It With: Eat these pickles as is or make them the basis of Quick Pineapple and Apple Salsa (page 141). The spears can be seared directly on a grill or cubed and skewered with vegetables and meat. Mix them with other fruit for a salad or dessert topping.

Fermented Rhubarb Pickles

Makes 1 quart

Prep time: 15 minutes, plus 30 minutes to 1 hour salting time

Curing time: 4 to 10 days

Rhubarb most often appears in desserts, mixed with plenty of sugar or sweeter fruit. But it gives another dimension to savory dishes. Rhubarb in vinegar would require even more sugar than dessert preparations to be palatable, so I ferment it. It takes a fair amount of salt to convince *Lactobacillus* bacteria to go to work, given rhubarb's low acidity and sugar content.

1½ pounds rhubarb stalks, cut into ½-inch slices (5¼ cups)

3 tablespoons Diamond Crystal kosher salt

1 (1-inch) piece peeled fresh ginger, finely sliced

2 teaspoons black peppercorns

1 teaspoon whole cloves

¾ teaspoon fennel seeds

6 cardamom pods, cracked

1. Put the rhubarb in a large bowl. Sprinkle with the salt, then toss until coated. Let sit for 30 to 60 minutes so that it starts to release liquid.

2. In the bottom of a clean quart jar, place the ginger, peppercorns, cloves, fennel seeds, and cardamom. Firmly pack the rhubarb and liquid into the jar. Cover the surface with cheesecloth; top with a weight and cover the fermenting vessel, preferably with an air lock. Let sit in a dark, cool place to cure.

3. After 24 hours, check that the surface layer is submerged. If it's exposed, add enough brine with a 3.5% concentration (see the Brine Concentration chart on page 12) to submerge the rhubarb.

4. Continue to check the fermentation daily, releasing air bubbles over the first 2 days. Top off with brine and skim off any filmy surface layer as needed.

5. Taste after 4 days of curing; continue fermenting for an additional 1 to 6 days as needed, until the pickles reach your preferred flavor. Store the finished rhubarb in its jar with a nonreactive lid in the refrigerator. As long as it stays submerged in its brine, it will keep for months.

Try It With: Serve fermented rhubarb on a relish tray or with Quick-Pickled Strawberries (page 169). Try it with stir-fried vegetables, spicy chickpeas over rice, or with fresh raw vegetables in a sushi bowl.

Quick-Pickled Strawberries

Makes 1 pint   **Prep time:** 10 minutes   **Curing time:** 12 hours

Strawberries and balsamic seem like a natural pairing, but the standard dark vinegar hides the beautiful red berries when they're combined in a jar. Swapping in white balsamic vinegar shows off the fruit; as the pickle sits, the berries' color will start to tinge the brine a light pink. Ripe berries will have the most flavor but soften faster than slightly underripe ones, so choose ripeness based on when you want to eat the pickle.

8 ounces fresh strawberries, hulled (1½ cups)

1 mint sprig (1½ teaspoons leaves)

⅔ cup white balsamic vinegar (6% acidity)

¼ cup water

1½ teaspoons vanilla sugar or granulated sugar

¾ teaspoon Diamond Crystal kosher salt

1. Cut any strawberries larger than 1 inch into halves or quarters.

2. Gently put the berries into a clean wide-mouth pint jar, tucking the mint against the side of the jar as you fill it. In a small measuring cup, whisk together the vinegar, water, sugar, and salt, stirring until the sugar and salt dissolve.

3. Pour the brine over the berries so that they are submerged but the brine is about ½ inch from the jar's rim. Screw on a nonreactive lid and refrigerate for at least 12 hours before eating. Leftover pickles can be stored in the refrigerator but are best eaten within 3 days.

Ingredient Tip: Strawberries need little additional sweetness even with vinegar, but a little sugar, especially when pre-infused with vanilla, balances the flavors well. An extra ¼ teaspoon of salt can enhance savory presentations, like salads and sushi rolls.

Vinegar-Pickled Watermelon Rind

Makes 1 quart

Prep time: 20 minutes, plus 30 minutes cooling time

Cook time: 1 minute
Curing time: 1 hour

If you grew up with a parent who canned, you likely encountered pickled watermelon rind, a frugal throwback that bears little resemblance to fruit. When processed in a boiling-water bath, the dark exterior skin remains tough and the red flesh becomes mush, so only the pale inner rind can be used. A quick pickle changes this: With a little flesh on the rind, each bite looks and tastes like watermelon.

1 (2-pound) watermelon

1 cup unseasoned rice vinegar (4.3% or higher acidity)

½ cup water

1 cup sugar

2½ teaspoons Morton pickling salt

1 (3-inch) cinnamon stick

4 slices peeled fresh ginger

2 whole cloves

1. Using a large sharp knife, cut the watermelon in half, then remove the center, leaving about ½ inch of red flesh on the rind (reserve the rest of the flesh for another use). Using a vegetable peeler, remove the rind's dark green skin. Cut the peeled rind into 1-inch squares.

2. In a large saucepan, bring the vinegar, water, sugar, and salt to a boil, stirring to dissolve the sugar and salt. And the cinnamon, ginger, and cloves, followed by the rind. Return the mixture to a boil, lower the heat, and simmer for 1 minute. Remove the pan from the heat; let the brine infuse for about 30 minutes, until cooled to room temperature.

3. Use a slotted spoon to transfer the rind and spices to a clean wide-mouth quart jar, packing it gently up to the shoulder of the jar. Ladle in the brine, submerging the rind. Screw on a nonreactive lid and refrigerate for at least 1 hour before eating. Leftover pickles are best eaten within 10 days.

Switch Things Up: For a savory pickle, use white wine vinegar, 1 fresh chile, and ¼ teaspoon mustard, dill, or cumin seeds, but keep the sugar to preserve and sweeten the otherwise neutral rind. If the pickled watermelon will sit less than a day, substitute ½ teaspoon ground cinnamon, ¼ teaspoon ground ginger, and pinch of ground cloves.

Fermented Watermelon Rind

Makes 1 quart   **Prep time:** 20 minutes   **Curing time:** 3 to 8 days

Pickled watermelon rind has a wartime history, perhaps as far back as the Civil War. Those early pickles were salt brined and then cooked with sugar and spices into a sweet relish. But you can simplify the process, and retain lovely probiotics, by eating just the crunchy fermented rind. Unlike Vinegar-Pickled Watermelon Rind (page 170), which reaches for the fruit's natural sweetness, this savory rind-only pickle builds a tangy, sour flavor.

1 (1½-pound) watermelon

2 cups unchlorinated water

2 tablespoons Diamond Crystal kosher salt

2 garlic cloves

⅛ teaspoon yellow mustard seeds

1 fresh dill head or 2 teaspoons dill seeds

1. Using a large sharp knife, cut the watermelon in half, then remove all the red flesh, reserving it for another use. Cut off one end of the watermelon so that you have a slice that will fit inside your fermenting vessel's opening; set this aside to use as a weight. Using a vegetable peeler, remove the rind's dark green skin and discard. Cut the peeled rind into 1-inch squares.

2. In a medium measuring cup, whisk together the water and salt, stirring until the salt dissolves.

3. In the bottom of a clean quart jar, put the garlic cloves and mustard seeds. Add the watermelon rind, packing it firmly but without bruising, up to the shoulder of the jar; tuck the dill head down the side. Cover the surface with the melon end-cut. Pour in the brine, submerging the rind; store extra brine in a small lidded jar. Top the melon with a weight if needed and cover the fermenting vessel, preferably with an air lock. Let sit in a dark, cool place to cure.

4. After 24 hours, start to check the fermentation daily, ensuring the pickles are submerged and skimming off any filmy surface layer. If they're exposed, add enough brine with a 3.5% concentration (see the Brine Concentration chart on page 12) to submerge the rind.

5. Taste after 3 days of curing; continue fermenting for an additional 2 to 5 days as needed, until the watermelon rind reaches your preferred flavor. Store the finished pickles in their jar with a nonreactive lid in the refrigerator. As long as they stay submerged in their brine, they will keep for months.

Switch Things Up: If you want to make both sweet Vinegar-Pickled Watermelon Rind (page 170) and tart Fermented Watermelon Rind, buy one larger melon and use half for each recipe. Pair them on a snack tray with nuts and cheeses, or top a green salad or avocado toast with the fermented rind.

Gravlax (Salt-Cured Salmon), page 178

Pickled Fish, Eggs, Beverages, and Other Odds and Ends

Blue Mule Ceviche (Citrus-Marinated Fish)

Serves 4

Prep time: 20 minutes, plus 15 minutes salting time

Curing time: 40 minutes to 5 hours

Named for our sailboat, the *Blue Mule,* this ceviche is a cruising-day favorite. The raw fish is denatured by citrus juice's acidity, so that it appears cooked. Besides high-quality ahi tuna, you can make this recipe with wild salmon, mahi-mahi, or halibut. Peruvians, who are said to be the masters of this dish, often use whatever trimmings and odd pieces of fish and shellfish are at hand; quality is more important than type.

¼ medium red onion, cut into paper-thin slices (¼ cup)

1¼ teaspoons Diamond Crystal kosher salt, divided

1 large (½-pound) steak ahi tuna or other meaty fish, cut into ½-inch cubes

¼ cup freshly squeezed or bottled lime juice (5% acidity)

¼ cup freshly squeezed or bottled lemon juice (5% acidity)

1 medium tomato, diced (½ cup)

2 garlic cloves, minced

½ red jalapeño pepper, minced, or ¾ teaspoon chile mash (from Scratch-Made Sriracha, page 130)

½ cup thinly sliced fresh basil

Freshly ground black pepper

1. In a small bowl, toss the onion with ¼ teaspoon of salt, then let it sit for about 15 minutes.

2. Drain the liquid from the onion slices, rinse them under cool water, then drain again before patting the slices dry with a dish towel.

3. In a clean, shallow, nonreactive container with a lid, combine the onion, fish, and remaining 1 teaspoon of salt. Cover with the lime and lemon juice and the lid, then let sit for 5 minutes.

4. Gently stir the ceviche with a spoon, making sure all the fish is coated with the marinade. Reseal the container and refrigerate for 30 minutes, until completely chilled.

5. Check the ceviche again for even marinating. If you prefer a firm exterior but translucent interior, remove the fish from the refrigerator; otherwise, return it to the refrigerator for another 3 to 5 hours, until the fish is opaque throughout and appears to be cooked (see Tip).

6. Strain off the excess marinade if desired and set it aside. Toss the fish mixture with the tomato, garlic, jalapeño, basil, and black pepper. Add the reserved liquid to the ceviche a tablespoon at a time to your preferred sauciness, then let it sit for 5 minutes. Serve immediately.

Ingredient Tip: You can prepare fully denatured fish 1 day in advance: After it has marinated for 3 hours, strain and reserve the marinade to slow the "cooking" process. Add the remaining ingredients up to 2 hours before serving, along with a little reserved marinade, if desired.

Herb and Pepper Ceviche (Citrus-Marinated Fish)

Serves 4 **Prep time:** 20 minutes **Curing time:** 40 minutes to 5 hours

Ceviche comes in many forms; styles that use fish, shrimp, various vegetables and fruits, and different acidic citrus juices can be found up and down the South and Central American coasts. The key factors are to use high-quality fish, like you would for sushi, and to ensure the citrus juice covers it. The final dish may look cooked, but technically it's been altered and preserved by the acidity of the citrus juice, not heat.

1 large (½-pound) steak swordfish or other meaty fish, cut into ½-inch cubes

6 scallions, white part only, thinly sliced (¼ cup)

1 teaspoon Diamond Crystal kosher salt

¼ cup freshly squeezed lime juice

½ large red bell pepper, finely chopped (½ cup)

½ cup fresh or frozen and thawed corn

½ jalapeño pepper, minced

1 tablespoon minced fresh cilantro

1 teaspoon minced fresh mint

½ teaspoon minced fresh flat-leaf parsley

1. In a clean, shallow, nonreactive container with a lid, combine the fish, scallions, and salt. Cover with the lime juice and the lid, then let sit for 5 minutes.

2. Gently stir the ceviche with a spoon, making sure all the fish is coated with the marinade. Reseal the container and refrigerate for 30 minutes, until completely chilled.

3. Check the ceviche again for even marinating. If you prefer a firm exterior but translucent interior, remove the fish from the refrigerator; otherwise, return it to the refrigerator for another 3 to 5 hours, until the fish is opaque throughout and appears to be cooked.

4. Strain off the excess marinade if desired and set it aside. Toss the fish mixture with the bell pepper, corn, and jalapeño; sprinkle with the cilantro, mint, and parsley and toss again. Add the reserved liquid to the ceviche a tablespoon at a time to your preferred sauciness, then let it sit for 5 minutes. Serve immediately.

Try It With: I typically serve ceviche with homemade sourdough pita bread, which can hold the fish's weight and soak up the marinade. You can also serve it with tortilla chips or even baked wonton crisps. Sweet potato cubes and chunks of corn on the cob are traditional accompaniments.

Gravlax (Salt-Cured Salmon)

Makes 1 pound   **Prep time:** 15 minutes   **Curing time:** 36 hours to 3 days

Scandinavians have long cured salmon with salt to keep spoilers at bay. Freezing wild salmon at a very cold temperature for several days, or buying commercially frozen fillets, kills potential parasites common in wild salmon. Although farm-raised salmon is less likely to contain parasites, I dislike the current standard practices and always choose wild-caught. Ensure delicious gravlax by selecting high-quality salmon and treating it like raw fish for sushi, keeping it cold and clean.

1-pound salmon fillet (such as coho or sockeye), skin on, defrosted

3 tablespoons Diamond Crystal kosher salt

2 tablespoons sugar

1½ teaspoons freshly ground black pepper

⅔ cup or more fresh dill fronds

1. Run your fingertips or the back of a knife over the fillet to check for small pin bones, removing them with tweezers. Cut the fillet in half crosswise into two pieces of equal length.

2. Lay a large piece of closely woven cheesecloth or butter muslin on a flat surface, then place the fillets, skin-side down, on the cloth, with two long edges touching and the thickest part of each piece at opposite ends.

3. In a small bowl, stir together the salt, sugar, and pepper. Sprinkle half of the salt mixture on each fillet, gently rubbing it into the flesh. Cover one fillet evenly with dill, then place the second fillet on top, creating a sandwich of fairly uniform thickness with the flesh sides together. Pack any salt mixture that came loose around the salmon.

4. Wrap the salmon in the cheesecloth, flipping and pulling slightly on the cloth and tucking in the loose ends with every turn (see Tip). Place the wrapped fish in a resealable bag, removing as much air as possible and folding extra plastic over the top of the salmon so that it is tightly enclosed. Place the bagged fish in a dish, ideally about the same size, and top with a second dish or other weight.

5. Refrigerate the salmon for at least 36 hours and up to 3 days, until the flesh feels firm with even color. Flip the bagged fish every 12 hours, taking care to keep the liquid in contact with the salmon.

6. Unwrap the fish and cut a piece from the tail end of one fillet. If this sample tastes too strong for you, rinse the fish under cold running water and then pat it dry.

7. To serve, use a sharp knife to separate the skin from the flesh, leaving the skin attached to any portion you won't be eating immediately. Slice the gravlax as thin as possible on the bias. Store the remaining fish by folding the gravlax-free skin over the cut surface and wrapping the salmon in waxed paper before enclosing it in a resealable bag and refrigerating it. It will keep for about a week.

Ingredient Tip: The goal during the curing time is to keep as much salmon as possible in its juices. I prefer cheesecloth because it can be stretched around the fish, lets the mixture "breathe," and is reusable, but you may prefer several layers of plastic wrap.

Escabeche-Style Fish (Fried and Pickled Fish)

Serves 4

Prep time: 20 minutes, plus 1 hour salting time

Cook time: 4 minutes
Curing time: 3 hours

Escabeche is a Spanish pickling technique most often used for fried fish. The acidic brine denatures the fish, like it does for Blue Mule Ceviche (page 176), so it needs only a quick sear. Although escabeche keeps for days in the refrigerator, the brine will continue to firm the fish, so I prefer to eat it the day it's made. The onion's color will turn the outer edge of the fish pink over time.

4 teaspoons Diamond Crystal kosher salt, divided

4 small steaks (1 pound) cod loin or other firm white fish

3 tablespoons sunflower oil

1 cup white wine vinegar (5% acidity)

4 teaspoons Mexican-Inspired Spice Blend (page 17)

4 garlic cloves, finely chopped

1 small red onion, thinly sliced (1 cup)

½ medium red bell pepper, sliced lengthwise (½ cup)

1 Fresno chile, finely chopped

1 tablespoon chopped fresh cilantro

¼ cup olive oil

1. Sprinkle 1 teaspoon of salt total on both sides of each piece of fish, then gently work it in with your fingers. Place the fish in a covered container and refrigerate for about 1 hour.

2. Pour any liquid off the fish, then rinse each piece under cool running water; let drain before patting dry.

3. In a large skillet, heat the sunflower oil over medium-high heat. Sauté the fish for no more than 2 minutes, flip, and cook for another 1 to 2 minutes, until cooked halfway through. Remove from the heat and let cool.

4. In a small measuring cup, whisk together the vinegar, remaining 1 tablespoon of salt, the spice blend, and garlic, stirring until the salt dissolves. Transfer the fish to a glass container with a nonreactive lid. Sprinkle with the onion, bell pepper, chile, and cilantro. Pour the brine over the mixture, followed by the olive oil. Cover the container and refrigerate for at least 3 hours before serving. It will keep for about a week in the refrigerator but is best eaten the first day.

5. To serve, let the fish sit at room temperature for about 10 minutes, until the oil liquefies. Transfer the fish with the vegetables and flavorings to a serving plate, flaking it into large pieces if desired, and drizzle with a couple of tablespoons of the brine.

Try It With: Escabeche makes a delicious summer main for four people or can serve more as a side dish or appetizer. Other vegetables can be used as fresh garnish, such as shredded spinach and scallions. Serve with fresh bread or tortilla chips to capture the sauce.

Swedish-Style Pickled Shrimp

Makes 1 quart

Prep time: 20 minutes, plus 15 minutes to 1 hour salting time

Curing time: 12 hours

This old recipe was adapted from a picnicking cookbook in my mom's collection and uses a whole-spice blend instead of fresh dill so that it can be served at both summer picnics and winter cocktail parties. The sweetness of an onion like the Walla Walla variety helps balance the slightly bitter spices, but you can substitute shallots, red onion, or even scallions as needed.

1 pound medium (41/50 count) or large (31/40 count) raw shrimp, fresh or frozen

1 teaspoon Diamond Crystal kosher salt

3⅔ cups water, divided

1 cup white wine vinegar (5% acidity)

½ sweet onion, thinly sliced (1¾ cups)

2 garlic cloves, thinly sliced

2 teaspoons Ultra Pickling Spice Blend (page 16)

1. Defrost the shrimp (if frozen) and peel.

2. In a medium bowl, toss the shrimp with the salt, cover the bowl, and refrigerate for 15 minutes to 1 hour.

3. In a medium saucepan, bring 3 cups of water to a boil. Add the brined shrimp and turn off the heat. Drain the shrimp through a colander after about 2 minutes, when they are just cooked through, then rinse them under cold running water until they are cool to the touch and drain again.

4. In medium measuring cup, whisk together the vinegar and remaining ⅔ cup of water.

5. In a medium bowl, combine the onion, garlic, and spice blend. Add the shrimp and toss to mix.

6. Pack the mixture into a clean wide-mouth quart jar. Pour the brine over the shrimp so that they are submerged but the brine is about ½ inch from the jar's rim. Screw on a nonreactive lid and refrigerate the shrimp for at least 12 hours before serving chilled. They will keep for a week or so in the refrigerator but are best eaten within a few days.

Try It With: The *Picnic Gourmet* recommends serving this shrimp as an appetizer on toothpicks and, if you're picnicking, storing it in a glass jar but transporting it in a plastic container. The shrimp pairs well with strong cheeses and fresh fruit; for a meal, toss it into a pasta salad.

Southern-Style Pickled Shrimp

Makes 1 quart

Prep time: 20 minutes, plus 15 minutes to 1 hour salting time

Curing time: 24 hours

Although you can buy precooked (a.k.a. rubbery and tasteless) shrimp, it's worth brining and cooking shrimp yourself, whether the shrimp is freshly caught or frozen. When I'm on the Pacific coast, nothing beats the shrimp pulled in pots from the ocean by my brother-in-law. But when inland at home in Montana, I buy only raw, individually frozen shrimp with the shell on; once peeled, I use the shells to make homemade seafood stock.

1 pound medium (41/50 count) or large (31/40 count) raw shrimp, fresh or frozen

4 teaspoons Diamond Crystal kosher salt, divided

3⅔ cups water, divided

1 cup apple cider vinegar (5% acidity)

½ teaspoon sugar

1 small red onion, thinly sliced (1 cup)

1 small lemon, thinly sliced (¼ cup)

¼ cup Chile and Tomatillo Hot Sauce (page 129) or other mild green hot sauce

2 tablespoons capers or Pickled Nasturtium Seeds (page 76)

1. Defrost the shrimp (if frozen) and peel.

2. In a medium bowl, toss the shrimp with 1 teaspoon of salt, cover the bowl, and refrigerate for 15 minutes to 1 hour.

3. In a medium saucepan, bring 3 cups of water to a boil. Add the brined shrimp and turn off the heat. Drain the shrimp through a colander after about 2 minutes, when they are just cooked through, then rinse them under cold running water until they are cool to the touch and drain again.

4. In medium measuring cup, whisk together the vinegar, the remaining ⅔ cup of water, remaining 1 tablespoon of salt, and the sugar, stirring until the salt and sugar dissolve.

5. In a medium bowl, combine the onion, lemon, hot sauce, and capers. Add the shrimp and toss to mix.

6. Pack the mixture into a clean wide-mouth quart jar. Pour the brine over the shrimp so it is submerged but the brine is about ½ inch from the jar's rim. Screw on a nonreactive lid and refrigerate the shrimp for 24 hours before serving chilled. It will keep for a week or so in the refrigerator but is best eaten within a few days.

Sweet Vinegar-Pickled Eggs

Makes 1 quart   **Prep time:** 20 minutes, plus   **Curing time:** 2 days
                          10 minutes cooling time

Pickled eggs have a long history of sitting behind a bar, just waiting for a customer to request a snack alongside a beer. Homemade pickled eggs must be refrigerated but can otherwise be as simply flavored as those bar-snack eggs or dropped into a brine that will add both flavor and color to the pickles. These slightly sweet pickled eggs, tinted by blackberries with a hint of orange flavor, may appeal to first-time pickled-egg eaters.

12 large hard-boiled eggs

1½ cups apple cider vinegar (5% acidity)

½ cup water

¼ cup sugar

2 teaspoons Morton pickling salt

1 (2-inch) piece orange peel

8 ounces fresh or frozen blackberries (1 cup)

1. Peel the eggs under cool running water, avoiding nicks and setting aside for another use any that lose their whites during peeling.

2. In a small saucepan, bring the vinegar, water, sugar, and salt to a boil, stirring to dissolve the sugar and salt. Remove the pan from the heat and add the orange peel; let the brine infuse for about 10 minutes, until cool enough to handle.

3. In a warm, clean wide-mouth quart jar, pack the eggs loosely, interspersing the blackberries as you go. Ladle the warm brine over the eggs so that they are submerged but the brine is about ½ inch from the jar's rim; store extra brine in a small lidded jar in the refrigerator. Screw on a nonreactive lid and immediately refrigerate the eggs for at least 2 days before eating, topping off the brine as needed to keep the eggs submerged. They will keep for weeks in the refrigerator but are best eaten within 10 days.

Ingredient Tip: To cook the eggs, bring a large saucepan of water to a boil, then lower the heat until bubbles just break the surface. Use a slotted spoon to gently add each egg, then raise the heat enough to keep the water bubbling; cook for 12 minutes. Immediately transfer each egg, using the slotted spoon, to a large bowl of ice-cold water and let sit for about 15 minutes, until cooled, before peeling.

Switch Things Up: Blackberries turn these eggs a gorgeous lavender that deepens to purple the longer they sit. Swap in blueberries for a similar hue or a slice of beet for a red tone.

Vinegar-Pickled Mustard Eggs

Makes 1 quart

Prep time: 20 minutes, plus 10 minutes cooling time

Cook time: 5 minutes
Curing time: 5 days

Part of the fun of pickling eggs is dropping them in a colorful brine; instead of disappearing with the shell, like Easter eggs, hues creep into the whites, spreading as the eggs sit. The whites also become rubbery and the yolks grow crumbly as they age, so find the curing time that suits you for color and texture. These eggs get a kick from the mustard that's balanced by the sugar.

12 large hard-boiled eggs (see Tip, page 183)

1½ cups white wine vinegar (5% acidity)

½ cup water

2 teaspoons sugar

1 tablespoon Morton pickling salt

2 garlic cloves, minced

4 teaspoons prepared stone-ground mustard or German-Inspired Spicy Mustard (page 151)

½ teaspoon yellow mustard seeds

½ teaspoon turmeric

⅛ teaspoon celery seeds

1. Peel the eggs under cool running water, avoiding nicks and setting aside any that lose their whites during peeling for another use.

2. In a small saucepan, bring the vinegar, water, sugar, and salt to a boil, stirring to dissolve the sugar and salt. Stir in the garlic, mustard, mustard seeds, turmeric, and celery seeds. Lower the heat and simmer for 3 to 5 minutes, stirring to distribute the spices. Remove the pan from the heat; let the brine infuse for about 10 minutes, until cool enough to handle.

3. In a warm, clean wide-mouth quart jar, pack the eggs loosely. Ladle the warm brine over the eggs so that they are submerged but the brine is about ½ inch from the jar's rim; store extra brine in a small lidded jar in the refrigerator. Screw on a nonreactive lid and immediately refrigerate the eggs for at least 5 days before eating, topping off the brine as needed to keep the eggs submerged. They will keep for weeks but are best eaten within 10 days.

Try It With: Pickled eggs make excellent snacks on their own or alongside meats and cheeses. They also pair well with soft pretzels. You can even turn them into extremely flavorful deviled eggs; I recommend tasting the yolk mixture before adding salt or any vinegar or other acid.

Strawberry-Balsamic Shrub

Makes 1½ cups

Prep time: 20 minutes, plus 24 hours macerating

Curing time: 1 day to 1 week

Don't think landscaping or Monty Python when a bartender offers you a shrub. She'll bring you a delicious beverage made from a concentrate of vinegar, fruit, and sugar, and perhaps alcohol and other enhancements. Shrubs were the precursors to Coca-Cola and other sodas, and in recent years they've been revived by savvy bartenders for colorful cocktails and house-made sodas. At home, you can store the concentrate in the refrigerator and enjoy it for months.

8 ounces fresh strawberries, hulled and quartered (1½ cups)

½ cup sugar

¾ cup apple cider vinegar (5% acidity)

¼ cup balsamic vinegar (6% acidity)

½ teaspoon black peppercorns

Seltzer for serving

1. In a large bowl, stir together the strawberries and sugar. Cover the container with a nonreactive lid and refrigerate for 24 hours, until the strawberries release their juice.

2. Strain the juice through a fine-mesh colander set over a large measuring cup, working in batches as needed.

3. In a medium measuring cup, whisk together the cider and balsamic vinegars, then pour them over the fruit, rinsing any undissolved sugar into the syrup; squeeze or press the strawberries as needed to remove as much liquid as possible. Reserve the fruit solids for another use.

4. Pour the liquid into a clean pint jar or 12-ounce bottle; add the peppercorns. Cap with a nonreactive lid, shake to distribute the flavors, and store the concentrate in the refrigerator for at least 1 day and ideally 1 week before using. It will keep for up to a year in the refrigerator. To serve as a shrub, combine 1 ounce of concentrate with 4 ounces of seltzer or more to taste.

Ingredient Tip: Some people may want a jewel-bright drink with pucker power and others may prefer sparkling water with a vinegary splash, so be prepared to adapt to each drinker's taste by leaving room in the glass. For a cocktail, replace 1 or 2 ounces of seltzer with gin or tequila.

Roasted Raspberry-Thyme Shrub

Makes 1½ cups

Prep time: 20 minutes, plus 8 hours macerating

Cook time: 25 minutes
Curing time: 1 day to 1 week

Shrubs can be adapted to many fruits, such as berries, stone or pome fruits, melons, or even tomatoes, and have the freshest flavor and color when the fruit remains uncooked. But macerating (letting sugar pull juices from the fruit) and then roasting draws out the most liquid and enhances the flavor of raspberries, cranberries, tangerines, and other tart fruit. Drink this shrub simply mixed with seltzer or lemonade, or serve it with gin and seltzer or gold rum and triple sec.

12 ounces fresh raspberries (2 cups)

1 cup sugar

8 thyme sprigs or 2 teaspoons dried thyme, divided

1 cup apple cider vinegar (5% acidity)

Seltzer for serving

1. Place the raspberries in a 9-by-13-inch baking pan and toss with the sugar and 6 thyme sprigs or 1½ teaspoons dried thyme. Cover the pan and refrigerate for from 8 hours to overnight, until the raspberries release their juice.

2. Preheat the oven to 400°F. Bring the pan to room temperature.

3. Roast the raspberries and their juice for about 25 minutes, until the berries float in juice. Remove the pan from the oven and mash the berries lightly with a large spoon. Strain the juice through a fine-mesh colander set over a large measuring cup, working in batches as needed. Pour the vinegar over the fruit, rinsing any undissolved sugar into the syrup; squeeze or press the raspberries as needed to remove as much liquid as possible.

4. Pour the liquid into a clean pint jar or 12-ounce bottle; add the remaining thyme. Cap with a nonreactive lid, shake to distribute the flavors, and store the concentrate in the refrigerator for at least 1 day and ideally 1 week before using. It will keep for up to a year in the refrigerator. To serve as a shrub, combine 1 ounce of concentrate with 4 ounces of seltzer or more to taste.

Ingredient Tip: After macerating and roasting, the remaining raspberry pulp will be mainly seeds. Although you can save these solids to puree into smoothies or stir into yogurt and granola, as you would for Strawberry-Balsamic Shrub (page 185), be prepared for some crunchy bites.

Switchel

Makes 1 quart   **Prep time:** 10 minutes   **Curing time:** 4 to 24 hours

Like the Strawberry-Balsamic Shrub and Roasted Raspberry-Thyme Shrub (pages 185 and 186), this classic beverage quenched the thirst of farmhands during hot late-summer and fall harvests. Today, a trend toward health tonics has renewed interest in switchel as a way to ingest its inflammation-reducing ginger. For the most health benefits, choose raw organic vinegar, organic Grade B maple syrup, and fresh organic ginger and lemon.

½ cup apple cider vinegar (5% acidity)

3 tablespoons maple syrup

1 tablespoon peeled, grated fresh ginger

½ lemon, cut lengthwise (see Tip, page 43)

3 cups water

1. In a clean quart jar, combine the vinegar and maple syrup, stirring until the syrup starts to dissolve. Add the grated ginger.

2. Squeeze the lemon juice into the jar, then add the lemon half. Fill the jar with water, screw on a nonreactive lid, and shake vigorously to distribute the contents.

3. Refrigerate the switchel for at least 4 hours and preferably 24 hours, shaking occasionally.

4. Remove the lemon half and shake the jar again before serving. Switchel will keep for 1 month or longer in the refrigerator.

Switch Things Up: Switchel is ready to drink as is. If the flavor is too strong straight from the jar, combine equal parts switchel and spring water and strain out the solids before you return it to the refrigerator. You can also sweeten it with another tablespoon of maple syrup.

Tepache (Fermented Pineapple Beverage)

Makes 1 gallon

Prep time: 20 minutes, plus 30 minutes cooling time

Curing time: 3 to 7 days, plus 1 hour refrigerated

Tepache is a fermented beverage made from the rind of pineapple, and it is popular throughout South and Central America. The size of the pineapple matters little, but choose one at full ripeness: Look for an evenly golden rind that gives when gently squeezed. If you smell the bottom point where the fruit was attached to the plant, a pineapple scent will confirm its ripeness.

1 (3½-pound) pineapple

3 quarts unchlorinated water

1 cup turbinado or brown sugar

1 (2-inch) stick of cinnamon (optional)

2 whole cloves (optional)

1. Twist the leaves off the pineapple, discarding them. Cut off the top and bottom with a large sharp knife. Stand the pineapple upright and cut off the peel in strips. Remove the remaining eyes with a small knife and cut the bottom into quarters. Place the bottom, eyes, and peel in a clean 1-gallon jar or crock. Reserve the pineapple flesh for another use (such as Pickled Pineapple, page 167).

2. In a large saucepan, bring the water and sugar to a simmer, stirring to dissolve the sugar. Remove the pan from the heat and add the cinnamon and cloves (if using). Let the brine infuse for about 30 minutes, until it has cooled to room temperature.

3. Ladle the brine over the pineapple trimmings, submerging the pieces. Cover the surface with the pineapple top before covering the fermenting vessel, preferably with an air lock. Let sit in a dark, cool place to cure.

4. After 24 hours, start to check the fermentation daily, ensuring the pineapple trimmings are submerged and skimming off any filmy surface layer. If they're exposed, add additional weight to submerge the pieces.

5. Taste after 3 to 5 days of curing; continue fermenting for an additional 1 to 2 days as needed, until the tepache reaches your preferred flavor.

6. Strain the juice through a fine-mesh colander set over a large measuring cup, working in batches as needed. Pour the liquid into three clean quart jars or 3 (32-ounce) bottles. Cap each with a nonreactive lid and store in the refrigerator for at least 1 hour before serving. If storing longer, burp the jars or bottles by loosening the lid every couple of days. It will keep for about 3 weeks in the refrigerator.

Switch Things Up: This highly effervescent beverage becomes drier the longer it carbonates. For a juicier tepache with fewer bubbles, loosen the cap and enjoy the drink within a few days. Serve it ice-cold on its own, with a splash of lime juice, or mixed with beer like a shandy.

Sweet Vinegar-Pickled Eggs, page 183

All about Altitude

Water at a higher elevation boils at a lower temperature. To compensate, processing times for water-bath canning must increase as elevation increases. Check out the chart on the following pages to find your altitude, or height above sea level; if your location isn't listed, you can likely find your elevation with a quick Web search. Then use this chart to make the necessary adjustments.

You can write the details here:

My altitude at _____ **is** _____.
(location)   (elevation in feet)

My altitude adjustment is _____ **minutes.**

Once you know this, just add this time to the one in the recipe whenever you attempt to can at this location.

ALTITUDE IN FEET	INCREASE PROCESSING TIME
0–1,000	No adjustment needed
1,001–3,000	5 minutes
3,001–6,000	10 minutes
6,001–8,000	15 minutes
8,001–10,000	20 minutes

Altitudes of Cities in the United States and Canada

UNITED STATES

STATE	CITY	FEET	METERS
Arizona	Mesa	1,243	379
	Phoenix	1,150	351
	Scottsdale	1,257	383
	Tucson	2,389	728
California	Fontana	1,237	377
	Moreno Valley	1,631	497
Colorado	Aurora	5,471	1,668
	Colorado Springs	6,010	1,832
	Denver	5,183	1,580
Georgia	Atlanta	1,026	313
Idaho	Boise	2,730	832
	Idaho Falls	4,705	1,434
Iowa	Sioux City	1,201	366
Kansas	Wichita	1,299	396
Montana	Billings	3,123	952
	Kalispell	2,956	901
	Missoula	3,209	978
Nebraska	Henderson	1,867	569
	Lincoln	1,176	358
	Omaha	1,090	332
Nevada	Las Vegas	2,001	610
	Reno	4,505	1,373

STATE	CITY	FEET	METERS
New Mexico	Albuquerque	5,312	1,619
	Santa Fe	7,260	2,213
North Carolina	Asheville	2,134	650
North Dakota	Bismarck	1,686	514
Ohio	Akron	1,004	306
Oklahoma	Oklahoma City	1,201	366
Pennsylvania	Pittsburgh	1,370	418
South Dakota	Rapid City	3,202	976
Texas	Amarillo	3,605	1,099
	El Paso	3,740	1,140
	Lubbock	3,256	992
Utah	Provo	4,551	1,387
	Salt Lake City	4,226	1,288
Washington	Spokane	1,843	562
Wyoming	Casper	5,150	1,570

CANADA

PROVINCE	CITY	FEET	METERS
Alberta	Calgary	3,600	1,100
	Edmonton	2,201	671
Ontario	Hamilton	1,063	324
Manitoba	Brandon	1,343	409
Saskatchewan	Regina	1,893	577
	Saskatoon	1,580	482

Resources

This section lists some of the tools and resources I use when pickling.

Canning Supplies

Be sure to select jars, lids, and rings designed specifically for home canning if you plan to process them in a boiling-water bath; see "Must-Have Tools," page 19, for more information.

- Ball (Kerr), FreshPreserving.com/products
- Fillmore Container, FillmoreContainer.com
- Le Parfait, LeParfait.com
- Roots & Branches (Victorio), VKPBrands.com/store/brand/roots-%26-branches

Fermenting Supplies

- Eden Farmhouse Essentials, EdenFarmhouseEssentials.com
- Fermentology, TryFermentology.myshopify.com
- Stone Creek Trading, StoneCreekTrading.com
- Yemoos Nourishing Cultures, Yemoos.com

Additional Storage and Food Prep Supplies

- Benriner mandoline, available from many local and online retailers
- iLIDS storage lids, IntelligentLids.com
- Mason Jar Lifestyle, MasonJarLifestyle.com
- Taylor food scale, TaylorUSA.com/shop/kitchen/food-scales/
- ThermoWorks pH meter and Thermapen, ThermoWorks.com

Additional Information

- Bone, Eugenia. *Well-Preserved*. New York: Clarkson Potter, 2009.
- Damrosch, Barbara. *The Garden Primer*. New York: Workman, 2008.
- Healthy Canning, HealthyCanning.com
- Katz, Sandor Ellix. *The Art of Fermentation*. White River Junction, VT: Chelsea Green, 2012.
- Kingry, Judi, and Lauren Devine, eds. *Ball Complete Book of Home Preserving*, rev. ed. Toronto, ON: Robert Rose, 2020.
- Krissoff, Liana. *Canning for a New Generation*, rev. ed. New York: Stewart, Tabori & Chang, 2016.
- MacCharles, Joel, and Dana Harrison. *Batch*. Vancouver, BC: Appetite by Random House, 2016.
- National Center for Home Food Preservation, NCHFP.uga.edu
- The Salt Cured Pickle, Facebook.com/groups/TheSaltCuredPickle
- Solomon, Karen. *Asian Pickles*. Berkeley: Ten Speed, 2014.
- *Twice as Tasty*, TwiceAsTasty.com
- USDA Complete Guide to Home Canning, 2015 revision, NCHFP.uga.edu/publications/publications_usda.html
- Ziedrich, Linda. *The Joy of Pickling*, 3rd ed. Beverly, MA: Quarto, 2016.

References

Avey, Tori. "History in a Jar: The Story of Pickles." PBS. September 3, 2014. PBS.org/food
/the-history-kitchen/history-pickles.

Etchells, J. L., T. A. Bell, and L. J. Turney. "Influence of Alum on the Firmness of
Fresh-Pack Dill Pickles." *Journal of Food Science* 37, no. 3 (May 1972): 442–445.
DOI:10.1111/j.1365-2621.1972.tb02659.x.

Frey, Malia. "Pickle Juice Nutrition Facts and Health Benefits." Verywell Fit.
Last modified March 15, 2020. VeryWellFit.com/pickle-juice-nutrition-fact
s-and-health-benefits-4164284.

Healthy Canning. "Crisping Pickles." Accessed April 26, 2020. HealthyCanning.com
/crisping-pickles.

———. "Steam Canning." Accessed April 18, 2020. HealthyCanning.com/steam-canning.

Henderson, Judy, and Carrie Thompson. "For Safety's Sake . . . Making Pickles in North
Carolina." North Carolina Cooperative Extension Service. Accessed April 25, 2020.
FBNS.ncsu.edu/extension_program/documents/foodsafety_making_pickles
_in_NC.pdf.

Ingham, Barbara H. "Homemade Pickles and Relishes." University of
Wisconsin-Extension. 2008. FoodSafety.wisc.edu/assets/preservation/B2267
_Pickles_08.pdf.

———. "Safe Preserving: Using a Steam Canner." University of Wisconsin–Madison,
Division of Extension. October 24, 2017. FYI.extension.wisc.edu/safepreserving
/2017/10/24/safe-preserving-using-a-steam-canner.

Kaplan, Kim. "It's Quite a Pickle to Be In." USDA blog. February 21, 2017. USDA.gov
/media/blog/2015/01/06/its-quite-pickle-be.

Katz, Sandor Ellix. *The Art of Fermentation.* White River Junction, VT: Chelsea
Green, 2012.

———. *Wild Fermentation.* White River Junction, VT: Chelsea Green, 2003.

Kingry, Judi, and Lauren Devine, eds. *Ball Complete Book of Home Preserving.* Toronto,
ON: Robert Rose. 2006.

Lynch, Francis T. *The Book of Yields: Accuracy in Food Costing and Purchasing,* 8th ed.
Hoboken, NJ: Wiley, 2010.

McGee, Harold. *On Food and Cooking,* rev. ed. New York: Scribner, 2004.

McGlynn, William. "The Importance of Food pH in Commercial Canning
Operations—Appendix 1: pH Values of Various Foods." Robert M. Kerr Food &
Agricultural Products Center, Oklahoma State University. 2016.

Miller, K. C. "Electrolyte and Plasma Responses after Pickle Juice, Mustard, and Deionized Water Ingestion in Dehydrated Humans." *Journal of Athletic Training* 49, no. 3 (May–June 2014): 360–367. DOI:10.4085/1062-6050-49.2.23.

National Center for Home Food Preservation. "Burning Issue: Canning in Electric Multi-Cookers." February 1, 2019. NCHFP.uga.edu/publications/nchfp/factsheets/electric_cookers.html.

———. "Burning Issue: Using Atmospheric Steam Canners." March 15, 2018. NCHFP.uga.edu/publications/nchfp/factsheets/steam_canners.html.

——— "How Do I? . . . Pickle." Accessed March 25, 2020. NCHFP.uga.edu/how/can6b_pickle.html.

Nolte, Kurt. "Sugar Snap Peas." Yuma County Cooperative Extension. Accessed March 26, 2020. CALS.Arizona.edu/fps/sites/cals.arizona.edu.fps/files/cotw/Sugar_Snap_Peas.pdf.

NY Food Museum. "Pickle History Timeline." Accessed March 18, 2020. NYFoodMuseum.org/_ptime.htm.

Petre, Alina. "Everything You Need to Know about Pickle Juice." Medical News Today. Last modified April 27, 2020. MedicalNewsToday.com/articles/318618.

Tyler Herbst, Sharon, and Ron Herbst. *The New Food Lover's Companion,* 5th ed. New York: Barron's. 2013.

US Department of Agriculture. "A Lab That Keeps Us All Out of a Pickle." *AgResearch Magazine* 62, no. 6 (July 2014): 4–9. AgResearchMag.ars.usda.gov/2014/jul/pickle.

———. *Complete Guide to Home Canning.* rev. ed. Washington, DC: USDA, 2015. PDF edition. NCHFP.uga.edu/publications/publications_usda.html.

US Food and Drug Administration. Compliance Policy Guide (CPG) Sec. 525.825. "Vinegar, Definitions—Adulteration with Vinegar Eels." Last modified March 1995. FDA.gov/regulatory-information/search-fda-guidance-documents/cpg-sec-525825-vinegar-definitions-adulteration-vinegar-eels.

University of Wisconsin-Extension. "Recommendations for Safe Production of Fermented Vegetables." July 2009. FoodSafety.wisc.edu/assets/pdf_Files/Fermented_Vegetables.pdf.

Ward, Christina. "Pickle Science: How to Master the Preserving Power of Acids." Serious Eats. Last modified November 1, 2019. SeriousEats.com/2017/08/preserving-pickle-cucumber-science-acidity.html.

Willmore, P., M. Etzel, E. Andress, and B. Ingham. "Home Processing of Acid Foods in Atmospheric Steam and Boiling Water Canners." *Food Protection Trends* 35, no. 3 (May–June 2015): 150–160. FoodProtection.org/publications/food-protection-trends /archive/2015-05home-processing-of-acid-foods-in-atmospheric-steam-and-bo iling-water-canners.

Ziedrich, Linda. "Real Lemon versus ReaLemon." *A Gardener's Table* (blog). April 19, 2011. AGardenersTable.com/real-lemon-versus-realemon.

———. *The Joy of Pickling,* 3rd ed. Beverly, MA: Quarto, 2016.

Index

C

Acknowledgments

I'm incredibly grateful to everyone who provided encouragement and ideas throughout this project—far too many to name. I'm particularly indebted to Erica von Kleist, who shared her business sense and creative juices from the word *book*. My taste-testing crew has my thanks for letting me invite myself to dinners bearing only pickles. I'm also grateful for the width and depth of the modern pickling cannon, including government and extension service resources and experts like Sandor Katz, Linda Ziedrich, and Eugenia Bone.

This book would not exist without TwiceasTasty.com readers and followers, who keep me writing and the blog growing. My thanks also go to Cecily McAndrews for her sharp eye and excitement for each new flavor, Caryn Abramowitz for her attention to detail, and the large crew at Rockridge Press who made the recipes look as delicious as they taste.

I never would have written a recipe without the lessons and support of my family, especially Mom, Dad, and Kristy (even though she wishes this was a cookie book). Above all, I'm grateful to George for his unwavering support, patience, and willingness to eat every single pickle I make.

About the Author

JULIE LAING has been a writer and editor for more than 25 years, with her career spanning jobs from music critic in Southern California, to advertising assistant in London, to editing positions in San Francisco and St. Petersburg, Russia. For the last 17 years, she has worked as a freelance writer and editor.

Julie is the creator and author of *Twice as Tasty*, a food blog focused on eating well year-round. She also teaches cooking workshops and prepares food as a personal chef. Julie lives in northwest Montana, where, with the help of her husband, George, she fills any spare space in their 500-square-foot cabin with homegrown and home-preserved food. When they're not at home, you'll find Julie and George sailing and eating well aboard the *Blue Mule*. You can find more delicious ways to make and use pickles at TwiceasTasty.com.

CPSIA information can be obtained
at www.ICGtesting.com
Printed in the USA
JSHW010003300721
17242JS00004B/4